# How to get your LAWN & GARDEN off drugs

A Basic Guide to Pesticide-Free Gardening in North America

## 2nd Edition

## Carole Rubin

Foreword by Robert Bateman

HARBOUR PUBLISHING

Published by
Harbour Publishing Co. Ltd., P.O. Box 219, Madeira Park, BC V0N 2H0
www.harbourpublishing.com

Edited by Shane McCune
Cover and page design by Charon O'Brien
Illustrations by Joanne Purich and Nick Murphy
Cover Illustration and map by Nick Murphy

Printed and bound in Canada
Printed on acid-free and chlorine-free paper, containing recycled post-consumer waste.

Harbour Publishing acknowledges the financial support from the Government of Canada through the Book Publishing Industry Program (BPIDP) and the Canada Council for the Arts, and the province of British Columbia through the British Columbia Arts Council, for its publishing activities.

THE CANADA COUNCIL | LE CONSEIL DES ARTS
FOR THE ARTS | DU CANADA
SINCE 1957 | DEPUIS 1957

National Library of Canada Cataloguing in Publication Data

Rubin, Carole
    How to get your lawn & garden off drugs : a basic guide to pesticide-free gardening in North America / Carole Rubin. — 2nd ed.

Previous ed. has title: How to get your lawn & garden off drugs: pesticide-free gardening for a healthier environment.
    Includes index.
    Includes bibliographical references and index.
    ISBN 1-55017-320-0

1. Organic gardening. 2. Lawns. I. Title.
SB453.5.R82 2003    635.9'64784    C2003-910094-4

For my mother, Isabel Rubin
and
In memory of
George Bayford
1920 - 2002

# ACKNOWLEDGEMENTS

The original version of this book would not have been possible without the assistance and encouragement of Julia Langer and Friends of the Earth, Canada.

Dr. Stuart Hill, Rod McRae, Ron Labonte, Ivy Wile, Dr. Linda Gilkeson, Arthur Beauregard, Stephen King, The Canadian Organic Growers Association, the Bio-Integral Resources Centre, University of California at Berkeley, Beyond Pesticides, Pesticide Action Network North America (PANNA) and many other individuals and groups provided encouragement, moral and technical support for both editions. Thanks to Ron Cameron, Michael Walker and Randy Wollen for their computer magic. Joanne Purich's wonderful illustrations still delight after all these years, and are beautifully complemented by the work of Nick Murphy.

To the troupers across Canada and the United States, known and unknown, who have been tirelessly encouraging their friends, families, neighbours, municipalities, states, provinces and countries to go pesticide-free, including Helen Jones, Maureen Reynolds, Mike Christie, Noha Faud, Kathleen Kelso, Kerry Berkenfohr and Valerie Chidwick, Cherry Dodd, Rebecca Turner, Maria Hunter, Steve Cohl, Lawns for Kids, The Raging Grannies, The Sierra Club, WWF Canada, Canadians Against Pesticides, Canadian Association of Physicians for the Environment (CAPE), Toronto Environmental Alliance, Beyond Pesticides, PANNA, etc.: thank you for your tireless work.

Keep on going. And make sure to take the time to treat yourselves and others as you would have the earth treated: with loving care and respect.

And lastly, many thanks to those who listened to all the voices of encouragement about a different way of approaching the "pest" issue and began to make changes in mind, heart and deed. We have come a long way since 1989. There's just more to do.

# TABLE OF CONTENTS:

# FOREWORD

To me, the most important song of the 20th century was Joni Mitchell's "Big Yellow Taxi". Its plea to farmers to stop using pesticides ("Give me spots on my apples/but leave me the birds and the bees") inspired my 1987 painting *Cardinal and Wild Apples*, a depiction of our own apple tree—which, of course, I do not spray.

When I give lectures I show a slide of the painting and ask audiences if they would buy apples with spots, maybe even pay more for them, if that meant supporting pesticide-free orchards. I say, "If your answer is no, guess what? Apple spots won't hurt you. If you close your eyes you won't even notice them. My grandmother ate apples with spots all her life and she did not die from apple spot."

In the 50 or so years that we have been spraying poisons on our lawns and gardens we have not eliminated one pest. Instead we have created many new pests, and at the same time we have wiped out many helpful organisms. Now our agricultural industry is hooked on pesticides and other chemicals. It is a destructive and expensive addiction that is hard to shake.

Thank goodness a growing number of dedicated people are finding healthy and cost-effective ways to kick this habit. Carole Rubin is one of these people. Since the early 1980s, she has followed in the footsteps of that great 20th-century heroine, Rachel Carson, whose book *Silent Spring* led to the North American ban on DDT. Carson was called an "environmental extremist" by the same powerful industrial forces that lobby and bully governments and scientists today. Of course, they were wrong and she was right. And now the bald eagle, peregrine falcon and brown pelican have been brought back from the brink of extinction. But the battle goes on and today the forces of poison are even wealthier and more insidious.

In their book, *Good News For a Change*, David Suzuki and Holly Dressel relate heartwarming tales of people the world over whose actions provide hope for a troubled planet. These people are part of a great and gradually emerging wave. They are working with nature for the good of human beings and all other living things. Carole Rubin and her book are a powerful part of this wave.

*How to Get Your Lawn and Garden Off Drugs* is a book whose time has come. It is a compelling and easy-to-use manual which could transform the relationship between human activity and nature.

Robert Bateman

*Renowned wildlife artist Robert Bateman (b. Toronto, 1930) has exhibited in countless galleries and museums throughout North America and has published several wildly successful art books—including his most recent, Birds.*

*Bateman's talent is matched only by his enthusiasm for environmental causes. In 1998 the US National Audubon Society named him one of the 20th century's 100 Champions of Conservation. In 1984 he was named Officer of the Order of Canada, the nation's highest civilian honour. He lives on Saltspring Island, British Columbia.*

# INTRODUCTION

When I wrote the first (Canadian) version of this book in 1989, I expected that the volume of pesticides used domestically would drastically decrease over the coming decade. After all, the federal governments of both Canada and the United States have finally stated that pesticides, by their very nature, were made to be toxic. Stories of pesticide contamination have abounded as information on alternatives multiplied. So I thought the public's dependence on these harmful chemicals would diminish.

Not so.

Herbicides, insecticides and fungicides continue to be used in unprecedented quantities in Canada and the United States. When a product is taken off the shelf by the government, no longer meeting the "acceptable risk" limit, three new pesticides come on line, with future impacts we cannot predict, until, 50 years from now, they too are possibly removed from the shelves. The United States Environmental Protection Agency (EPA) estimates that 46 million kg (102 million pounds) of chemicals were applied to US lawns and gardens last year and they expect that number to increase by six percent every year.

The legacy? Pesticide residues can be found in every living thing. The polar ice cap—about as remote as you can be from a garden—contains DDT, among other man-made chemicals. There is not a water body, animal, tree, bird, fish or human on the planet that does not have some pesticide contamination.

And the "pests?" They keep coming back. Bigger, stronger, immune to chemicals they have learned to adapt to. Heck, they eat 'em for breakfast. Pesticide manufacturers depend on it. So the problem is never solved, the toxic money is perpetually made and the environmental destruction continues.

The good news is that some people are taking the time to learn about alternatives to pesticides. Alternatives that design pests out of the equation in the first place or deal effectively with a problem when it does arise. Alternatives that do not harm beneficial organisms, or the soil itself. Alternatives that are not potion based, but are instead based upon cultural practices that build the soil, producing hardy plants that are pest-resistant. Alternatives that are not toxic to humans or wildlife and that will not contaminate our groundwater.

Even more startling, municipalities across North America are implementing or considering "no cosmetic use pesticide by-laws," encouraging their residents to learn about the alternatives. Unheard of 13 years ago—and savagely opposed today.

Governments that have banned substances they deemed too risky, passed no-pesticide by-laws, or that are *considering* no-pesticide legislation, must deal with threats of multi-million dollar lawsuits brought forward by pesticide manufacturers—some of the deepest pockets in the world. This is a tragedy. Governments should not have to go broke defending the right to draft environmentally sound by-laws that protect human health. Governments should not have to defend the right to ban substances they deem too high a risk.

So this book is for individuals who want to learn how to do something about this state of affairs in an area they can control: their own yards. This book is for those who want to learn about those alternatives and put them to use in their gardens and on their lawns, knowing they are doing something to restore and protect their own small domain. Hopefully this book will make its way, neighbour to neighbour, throughout whole communities, so that we can say we did better at the end of the next decade.


Psst. Pass it on...

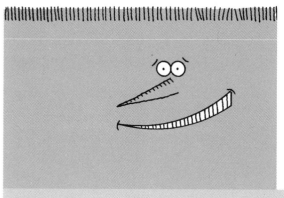

1

# PESTICIDE MYTHS AND HISTORY

S ince the Second World War, chemical fertilizers and pesticides have been promoted as the technological cure-all for plant nutrition and the "management" of plant insects, weeds and diseases.

Today, after 50 years of chemical gardening and lawn care, we can find pesticide and fertilizer residues in our water, fisheries, wildlife species, soils—and ourselves. Now, we are looking for ways to reverse that pollution. We are looking for ways to enrich soils, which have been depleted of organic material and sometimes reduced to a sterile toxic sand as a result of repeated chemical treatments.

## CHEMICAL FERTILIZER
### The not so healthy 'quick-fix'

Fast-releasing chemical fertilizers send a rush of nitrogen into the soil. But in order to make use of the nutrients in this fertilizer, soil microbes must take energy from organic matter. The organic matter is gradually depleted and the soil becomes progressively more lifeless.

The less organic matter in the soil, the more chemical fertilizer it needs to support plant life. A cycle of chemical dependency is established.

Chemical fertilizers do not improve or feed the soil: they are designed for immediate uptake by the plants. This is incredibly inefficient and short-sighted, leading to highly nitrogenized, weakened plants and poorly nourished, depleted soils that do little more than hold the plants upright.

Furthermore, chemical nitrogen has short-lived benefits for the plants themselves. It is highly water-soluble and it quickly leaches away into the water table under the soil, polluting it and leaving the plants wanting more. Addicted plants. Organically poor soil speeds this leaching process.

Overuse of chemical fertilizers can also kill beneficial organisms in the soil, lowering your plants' defences against harmful diseases and insects. Studies at Cornell University have shown fewer predatory insects on collards fertilized with manure than on those fertilized with synthetic fertilizers.

Overuse of chemical fertilizers also disrupts the pH balance of your soil, making it too acidic and, in some areas, salty.

**More Than You Bargained For**

What many people don't realize is that when "fertilizers" are purchased at the store, many come pre-packaged with herbicides; thus the "weed" in "Weed & Feed." Read the label on that synthetic fertilizer carefully: not only will you find ingredients that do little to support the soil, you may also find toxic pesticides that will harm beneficial organisms in the soil you are trying to keep healthy. Bad idea all around.

## CHEMICAL PESTICIDES
Two truths and a toxic arsenal

### Truth one:
Chemical pesticides are the only class of chemicals *made to be toxic*. They need to be toxic to achieve their desired effect. Just ask the governing agencies that register them for use. I did, and this was the response of the Pest Management Regulatory Agency, Health Canada:

> Although their biological effects are what make most pest control products valuable to society, these effects can also pose a risk to human and environmental health. (PMRA /About PMRA 2001-08-09)

### Truth two:
The governments of Canada and United States repeatedly insist that registration of a pesticide for use under their respective legislation *does not guarantee or even imply safety*, or—get this—*effectiveness*.

"The PMRA is responsible for providing safe access to pest management tools, while minimizing risks to human and environmental health." And: "The Pest Control Products Act (the legislation that allows products to be used in Canada) regulates the use of substances that *claim* to have pest control use." (My italics.)

Finally, the PMRA's stated mission is "to protect human health and the environment *by minimizing the risks associated with pest control products*, while enabling access to pest management tools ..." (My italics.)

So, registration is about "minimizing the risks" associated with products that claim to work. Got it?

Many chemical companies, the university programs they fund and the landscaping companies that use and sell chemicals, repeatedly tell customers that pesticides are "safe." Why, they'd eat 'em by the cupful. They go on TV, publish ads and articles in major publications, extolling the "safety" of the products.

They are breaking the law when they do so.

Legally, one can only claim that "risks associated with pest control products will be reduced when the product is used according to label instructions." (*Agriculture Canada, 1990.*)

Ever read a pesticide label? Ten to 50 pages of exceedingly minute print full of technical language. No one I canvassed in my community had read more than a few words on the labels of the products they use. So how could the product be applied in a way that would reduce risk? No one who hired a lawn-care company to dose their yard knew *anything* about the products applied to their immediate environment—not even which chemicals were used. So here's a bit of information we could all use:

The General Accounting Office of the Congress of the United States is continually publishing reports about false claims of safety made by manufacturers and industrial users of pesticides (read: lawn-care companies). Hefty fines are levied and guess what? The fines are gladly paid and the false claims of safety continue. It's all a part of doing business.

## PESTICIDE HISTORY
### Killers from the get-go

Chemical pesticides were first formulated during the Second World War as agents of chemical warfare, central nervous system disruptors to be used on humans. When it was discovered that some of these products defoliated the broad-leaved trees at spray sites, a whole new application was born as the warfare between humans died down. The "nerve gases" left over could be used in agriculture to kill broad-leaved weeds in crops.

Research and development of chemical herbicides, insecticides, fungicides and other toxic agents has since produced thousands of products for use in agriculture, forestry, fisheries, structural pest-control and home gardens and lawn care.

A multi-billion-dollar industry has ballooned in the last five decades, led by the companies who were first commissioned to come up with chemicals that would kill humans in war.

Thousands of these products hit the shelves, available to farmers, foresters and homeowners alike before tests for human health and environmental harm were even thought of.

In the past 20 years, both Canada and the United States have agreed that testing requirements for pesticides needed to be improved. In the early 90s, new requirements were introduced in both countries, but most of the thousands of products already on the shelves have yet to be tested to meet these requirements. In fact, more than 70 percent of the pesticides registered for use in Canada as this book goes to press have not been fully tested but are still registered, sold, bought and used in the millions of pounds every day.

No wonder the governments of both countries state that registration is not a guarantee of safety.

## PESTICIDES' HIDDEN LITTLE SECRET
'Formulants'

Just what's *in* those pesticide bottles, anyway? The label lists only the "active ingredient." That may be only one of hundreds of chemicals in any one bottle. So what else is in there?

We don't know and will never be allowed to know, if the chemical companies have their way. Hey, we might steal the formula and make millions. So the identities of the formulants are protected by law from the public's eyes. That is considered "Confidential Business Information."

So who *does* know?

Since 1993, manufacturers are required to disclose to the Canadian and US governments the identities of all ingredients in new pesticides that they want to have registered and the government agencies responsible for allowing the bottles on the shelf are supposed to read every item on the list as part of the registration process. An improvement in law, but in reality, totally undoable when the workload of the few people working on these projects is considered.

And, in reality, companies contract out portions of their products and may not know, themselves, what's in the bottle.

And what about the products registered before 1993, which are still being made and sold by the millions of pounds? Our governments don't know what's in those formulas, either.

Why is that a problem? Because any one of 5,000 substances can be legally added to the "active ingredient" in the bottle you purchase, to help the combined chemical soup spread more evenly, stick to foliage, etc. Unfortunately, in the 1980s, DDT, various other banned chemicals and in one instance I know of, *toxic waste* were illegally added to some pesticides as additives.

Makes some of us wonder just who Confidential Business Information legislation really protects.

Bottom line: The bottle on the shelf is a pig in a toxic poke, if you will. We do not know what we are buying or using on our lawns and gardens.

More bad news about the genie(s) in the bottle. Most of the tests required for registration are conducted on the one chemical identified as the "active ingredient," not the entire mixture that you buy in the bottle. And that active ingredient often only makes up a very small portion of what you are buying—in some instances, less than two percent. And yet when independently tested, the active ingredient has been found in some cases to be *less* toxic than the secret additives.

## HOW CHEMICAL PESTICIDES 'WORK'

Synthetic chemical pesticides are formulated to try to kill "target" species, be they weeds, rodents, insects, or diseases. The problem is, as Pesticide Action Network North America stated so brilliantly in the early 80s, "pesticides don't know when to stop killing." A chemical formula cannot distinguish a "good" broad-leafed plant from a "bad", or an aphid from a ladybug. Everything is wiped out.

So an insecticide applied to target aphids will also kill aphids' natural predator, the ladybug, along with millions of other beneficial insects and organisms in your lawn and garden that keep the natural balance of predation in check and help your soil stay fertile. It will also kill or damage aquatic animals in the water system it contaminates with the next rain or sprinkling, get into our bodies when we drink the water or eat the fish, and evaporate into the air from our lawns to form clouds that blow everywhere on earth (polluting the fatty tissues of arctic polar bear cubs born this year) and pass on to our children in mothers' milk and so on.

If there's one thing we have learned since 1989, it is that the entire planet is our neighbourhood. Everything we do affects the whole shebang.

## THE HORMONE FACTOR
Involuntary sex change, anyone?

If the realization that pesticides don't know when to stop killing isn't bad enough, there is growing evidence, according to the World Health Organization, that pesticides may be contributing to declining human sperm counts and that endocrine disrupting chemicals (EDCs) in pesticides have adversely effected the reproductive organs and behaviours of some wildlife species. It seems that many adult male alligators in the Florida Everglades have unformed or malformed reproductive organs, caused by exposure to EDC's, which mimic the female hormone estradiol. Exposure in infancy and childhood, both critical developmental periods, is especially harmful.

Exposure to pesticides may be turning males into females.

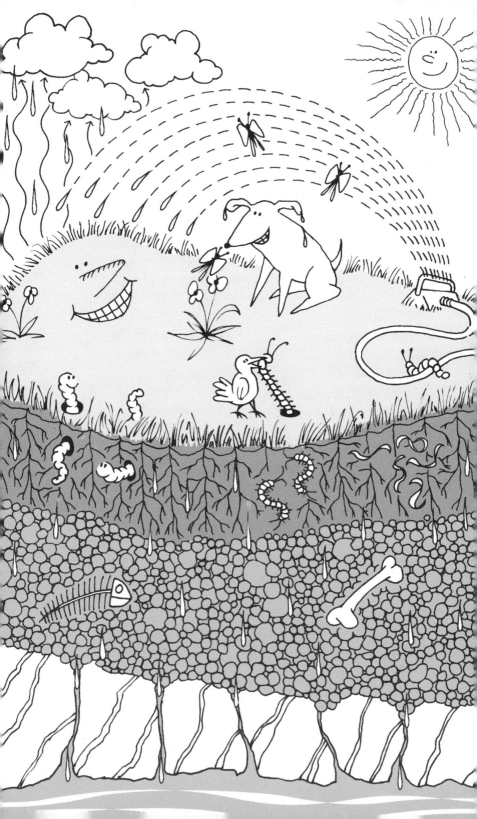

## ONE PLUS ONE EQUALS...?
The 'chemical soup'syndrome

Here's another issue that is never addressed by chemical manufacturers, landscape companies who use chemical pesticides, or by governments who register them: synergy.

What happens to the effects of a pesticide, or one of its ingredients, when it is mixed with another chemical intentionally, as in a formula, or unintentionally, as in a cocktail of several pesticides sprayed on an orchard or garden? How many pesticides are registered for use on your yard? What happens when they are all used in one week or day and they get together and party? Is the resulting soup more toxic to humans than the individual chemical compound? More toxic to wildlife? No one knows and no one who makes the chemicals or the laws that "control" them is asking.

## ENVIRONMENTAL FATE
That great pesticide heaven in the sky

Then we have the issue of "environmental fate." Many pro-pesticide types argue that the chemicals break down, dissolve and disappear in so many days or weeks. Gone, no problem.

Excuse me? Nothing we create "goes away" (see illustration, p.18). A pesticide may leach into local water systems, evaporate and float away in clouds, break down into smaller or different molecules, but who are these molecules when they are at home and what effects do they have on us and the living things around us? Again, these questions are not considered during registration.

## DO THEY WORK?

A last truth about pesticides: They don't work. Pesticide manufacturers depend on it. Think about it: if one of the many chemicals in the bottle actually manages to knock off the "pest" for awhile, all you have to do is wait. Those little beasts soon reassert themselves, but this time around, they are stronger and more and more often immune to the chemical. This time there are no natural predators left alive to deal with the problem, because they were killed by the last generation of chemicals—along with millions of other insects and organisms that were innocent bystanders. More, stronger, newer pesticides are needed. Once again, a cycle of dependency is established that has nothing to do with lawn and garden health and everything to do with profits.

## A POTION IS A POTION IS A POTION...

Even organic pesticides—those seemingly innocuous potions that have been the rage of organic gardeners (mea culpa) for the past couple of decades—don't know when to stop killing.

They are not target- or species-specific, either. Insecticidal soap will harm any insect it comes into contact with, be it aphid or ladybug. Garlic spray, if made too strong, will actually burn the leaves of plants it is applied to. Pyrethrin, made from the chrysanthemum plant, has been found to harm non-target species, including humans. And *Bacillus thuringiensis* (Bt)? Who knows? And isn't that the whole point?

And then there's the fact that potions—even organic ones—never solve the problem that brought the "pest" to your lawn or garden in the first place. They are used to attack the symptom—the weed, the insect, the disease—not to remedy the cause. So the potion must be applied again, because the conditions are still present, attracting the "pest" for a return engagement.

Well, it's no longer acceptable to use a "less toxic" remedy. Less toxic to whom? If it's still toxic to ladybugs, it's out of here. Kills the beneficial micro-organisms I have so carefully made a home for in my soil? Forget it. If pests are to be dealt with, they must be *designed* out of your yard. End of story.

And that's what you'll find in this book: design-based solutions to "pest" problems.

## PESTICIDE-FREE BY DESIGN

2

Y ou can have a gorgeous yard, beautiful flowers, nutritious vegetables and healthy trees and shrubs without the use of synthetic pesticides or "organic" potions.

The alternative regimen may seem more labour-intensive than pulling a bottle off the shelf, dosing your yard every few days and walking away, or hiring a company to do it with a "cocktail," but the rewards are worth it. If you are unable to do the labour yourself, hire a local teenager, or lawn/garden care company that follows the principles listed below.

This keeps your dollars in the community, not in the pockets of the major multi-national corporations that make pesticides and other nasty things. If your landscaping company has not yet "gone organic," talk to them about it. They'll find more clients than they dreamed of. The Organic Landscape Alliance in Ontario, Canada (see **Resources**) have more clients than they can accommodate and the good news is, demand for pesticide-free lawn and garden care is spreading. And if your company still won't offer the program you want, shop elsewhere.

You may pay more for an organic regimen in the first couple of years, because of the hands-on maintenance program, but after that time, you will actually spend the same, if not less, than resorting to the chemical soup approach. If your contractor continues to charge you more after a few seasons, check it out. A well fed, well maintained crop should become less labour-intensive as time goes by.

So here we go!

Pesticide-free lawn and garden care relies on designing pests out of your yard with appropriate plant selection, healthy soil, appropriate tolerances levels, sound cultural practices and proper maintenance. In other words, good basic horticulture.

## THE SEVEN PRINCIPLES OF ORGANIC CARE

### 1. Plant selection
What works, where it works

In order to get the maximum pleasure out of your yard and to have the minimum amount of hassles, it is important to design your lawn and garden to fit your exact location. Even if you have a yard that is well established, look around, discover what your plants are telling you and make the appropriate changes.

# A Very Important Word About 'I P M'

Integrated Pest Management, or IPM, is the buzz-word most recently rendered meaningless by anyone and everyone in the "crop protection" business. It was introduced in the late 1980's to define a multi-pronged approach to pest control that was supposed to follow certain stages, most of which were outlined in the first edition of this book:

1. appropriate plant selection

2. healthy soil

3. good horticultural and cultural practices

4. least-toxic remedies (read "potions," biological remedies and introduced beneficials) when pests persist and

5. chemical pesticides as a last resort. (Of course, I never endorsed this.)

However, when someone today claims to provide an IPM program, you have no idea what they will actually do to your lawn or garden— unless you ask for details. *So ask.*

After you have read this book, get an IPM definition, in writing, from the service providers you are considering hiring. Ask them to list which controls their company uses to deter pests. Ask them to list any organic or synthetic pesticides they may use. Ask them to list any cultural or horticultural practices they use as pest control. Which fertilizers do they use? How they would modify your yard to prevent problems. Ask, ask, ask.

Some companies believe IPM means synthetic pesticides are one of the tools they should use from the get-go for some (if not all) pests, because they are sure that's the only remedy. And all landscape care providers have a different take on "last resort." So ask.

And remember, the only true "pesticide-free program" is, well, pesticide-free.

For example, say you live in the Pacific Northwest. That cactus your Aunt Annie in Arizona sent you last Christmas will rot by New Year's despite copious amounts of fungicides because it is the wrong plant, in the wrong region and site, for your growing conditions.

Ditto trying to bring that hibiscus on your move to New Mexico from Pennsylvania. Won't work!

Most gardening problems can be avoided by selecting plants that like the climate and soil where you live. Less stress to the plants = fewer problems with pests.

Another example: If you have a steep slope with poor soil and are trying to establish a lawn on it, give it up. The water so badly needed by 20-cm (8-in.) grass roots will just run down the hill, leaving the grass plants thirsty and weak. Once they are weak, you know who will come knocking. So on steep slopes, plant a more suitable ground cover.

Take conventional turfgrass lawns and shade: Forget about it! Conventional turfgrasses will simply not do their best in deep shade.

And please, don't be cutting down your shade plants to provide enough exposure for your lawn; in the coming years, we are going to need all the shade we can get. Instead, take up what's left of the struggling lawn and plant a shade-lover in the shade.

## Bug-Eating Birds

Certain plants attract birds that feed mainly on weeds and insects. These birds belong to the Fringillidae family, which includes cardinals, purple and house finches, buntings, crossbills, grosbeaks, goldfinches, towhees, juncos and the dozens of varieties of native sparrows. You want these birds living and feeding in your yard.

Flowers such as sunflowers, marigolds, cosmos, amaranthus and portulaca all attract winged pest control. Birds are attracted to the seeds of these flowers, but during the spring and summer they will move on to consume great quantities of insects and weeds. The flowers must be allowed to go to seed to ensure attendance, so don't whisk away blooms as soon as they begin to droop. Plants listed not only attract birds, they also go to seed gracefully, so to speak.

Even better, plant native grasses, flowers, shrubs, trees and vines that like your soil and climate just the way it is, wherever possible in your yard. Replace all your struggling, pest-prone exotics with natives that will need no water after their first year. You'll also be attracting birds and butterflies that feed on lawn and garden "pests."

You can provide food and shelter for bug-eating birds, restore native habitat and reduce your maintenance to zero by planting grasses, flowers, vines, shrubs and trees that are native to your area.

**California:** Plant toyon (California holly) to attract warblers, thrashers, towhees and sparrows and California buckeye to attract woodpeckers.

**Pacific Northwest**: Kinnikinnik and salal provide food and shelter for towhees, thrashers and sparrows. Red-flowering currant, my all-time favourite, brings warblers, thrashers, sparrows and, as a bonus, the first hummingbirds of the season to the yard.

**Southwestern Deserts**: Plant claret cup cactus, pink fairy duster, brittlebush, chuparosa, Joshua trees, ocotillo and honey mesquite. Bobwhites, quail, songbirds, warblers, orioles, goldfinches, flickers and nesting birds will move in and stay for the food you have provided them.

**Mountains and Basins**: Plant sideoats grama, datil, rabbitbrush, golden currant, quaking aspen and pinyon pine to make a home for meadowlarks, finches, pine siskins, owls, swallows, bluebirds, pinyon jays and quail.

**Great Plains**: Plant blue grama grass (that great lawn alternative), little bluestem, buffalo grass (the other great lawn alternative), Indian grass, chokecherry, downy hawthorn and eastern cottonwood. You'll be making homes for grosbeaks, finches, meadowlarks, juncos, sparrows, songbirds, robins, towhees, cedar waxwings and orioles.

**Northeast**: Plant bearberry, eastern redbud, sassafras, red osier dogwood and paper birch. Grouse, songbirds, blue jays, nesting birds, grosbeaks, thrushes, cedar waxwings, pine siskins, phoebes and woodpeckers will move in and eat their fair share of lawn and garden pests.

**Southeastern Coastal Plains**: Honeysuckle, flowering dogwood and sour gum trees will bring cardinals, catbirds, bluebirds, bobwhites, mockingbirds, robins, finches, flickers, grosbeaks and buntings to your yard.

For more on native plants and birds they attract, see *How To Get Your Lawn Off Grass* (C. Rubin, Harbour Publishing).

## 2. Soil
Deep and well fed

Once you've chosen your species wisely, the next requirement for healthy plants is deep and well-fed soil.

Your soil *must* be deep enough to provide for full root growth. Full root growth is essential for strong plants and strong plants are essential to resist pests.

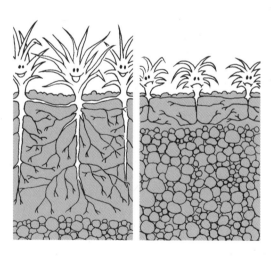

For example: turfgrasses such as Kentucky bluegrass need 20 cm (8 in.) of soil for full root extension. Plant something else if you have only 7.5 cm (3 in.) of topsoil, no matter how well fed. Otherwise, the roots will be too short to support the plant. They will be cramped, malformed and generally stressed, leading to plants that are less resistant to drought, heat, cold, diseases, insects and opportunists such as broad-leaved weeds.

Soil must also be well fed to build healthy, pest-resistant plants, be they flower, fruit, shrub, tree or grass blade. Your soil will likely need a diet of organic amendments that, unlike synthetic chemical fertilizers, are slow-releasing, long-lasting, beneficial to healthy soil organisms and more closely match the soil's own structure.

## 3. Tolerance levels
### How to make friends with ladybugs and dandelions

North Americans have a strange obsession about "pests," far out of proportion to the damage they actually cause. Did you know that only one percent of insects are actually harmful to your plants? And that millions are beneficial to your plants because they eat other predators, or aerate the soil, or make nutrients available to plant roots?

Insects are amazing and amazingly beautiful. Pick up a copy of a field guide (see **Further Reading**) that has gorgeous colour plates of insects from your neck of the woods, or thumb through one at the library. You'll find incredible colours, shapes, mating habits and food preferences. As you expose yourself to these images and learn more about insect habits, hopefully you will be able overcome your fears, or at the very least, refrain from passing them on to the next generation.

Same with "weeds." A weed is a plant growing where you don't want it to be. End of story. Actually, beginning of a story:

A friend of mine from Ottawa house-swapped with a family in rural France for a year in the early 1980s. Thinking she was doing the family a favour, she diligently dug all the dandelions out of their yard, roots and all, with a trowel. It took her months. Once they were back in their own countries, the French family phoned my friend in Ottawa. They were furious. She had destroyed heirloom plants, passed on for seven generations, used for wine and salad greens. Cultural ignorance was cursed, arrogance mocked. A lawsuit was threatened. Gives us a different perspective, n'est-ce pas?

Why *are* North Americans dead-set against dandelions, anyway? What is it that makes a person feel they are letting down the community if the yellow beauties, so high in vitamins A and D, are found in their lawn? Why is a dull, boring, green carpet a prerequisite for status and self esteem? Why must our yards look exactly the same, no matter where in North America we live? Why must they mimic golf courses? *Why don't we just nail down some indoor-outdoor carpeting and have done with it?*

What if the new status symbol in this millennium was a yard full of clover and dandelions? Ditto buttercups. How can our children play the "do you like butter?" game without them? What's wrong with us, that we need to kill off what grows naturally to make our yards *look* like indoor-outdoor carpeting?

Weeds, insects and diseases tell us valuable things. Dandelions, for example, indicate dry, poorly nourished soil, poor watering and mowing practices. How would you know it's time to aerate, add compost and improve your maintenance techniques without them? Clover indicates low nitrogen and dry soil. Ivy means your lawn is wet and shaded. Chinch bugs like thatch and hot, dry soil fed with too much nitrogen. Get the picture?

Pests can tell us what we need to do to improve the health of our soil to support the plants we want to grow. They are indicators of poor maintenance or inappropriate plant selection. Listen to your insects and weeds.

## 4. Maintenance
A little work goes a long way

Most garden problems—up to 80 percent of them, some turf researchers say—are caused by poor maintenance. So it makes sense to learn what works and doesn't when it comes to growing stress-free, healthy plants and to abandon old habits that no longer apply. For example, part of the esthetic of the past two decades has dictated cutting the lawn every three days or so to a height of 1.3 cm (½ in).

Well, the US Department of Agriculture does exactly the same thing when it wants to attract a lawn disease to study. Turns out close mowing stresses the grass plants so much, diseases are just waiting for the fumes to die down before moving in.

The same is true of mowing with dull blades, watering too shallowly too often, feeding at the wrong time of year, etc. So read up on correct maintenance practices for your lawn, in Chapter 4-6, and prevent 80 percent of your problems.

## 5. Monitor
### Take a walk on the tame side

Simply looking at your plants on a regular basis will help you to spot problems early. The earlier the better, in terms of turning the problem around.

See a brown spot on the lawn? Look in Chapter 4 to find out what to do next. See an insect in your vegetable garden you don't recognize? Capture and identify it before taking any action. See eaten leaves but no insect? Come back in the evening with a flashlight and check it out. Or take a leaf to a reputable nursery. Mould or fungus on your lawn? Watch the area after the next rain. Is the soil allowing the water to drain, or making it sit for hours, breeding problems? Are you watering too late in the day, insuring a cool, wet, dark breeding ground?

The reason it's so important to look at your yard is so that you will spot changes, begin to identify problems and learn which "pests" (human, insect, plant or viral) are the cause, before you reach for a toxic "remedy."

## 6. Identify the problem
Is it pest or guest?

Only one percent of insects actually harm plants that we grow in our yards, so it is important to identify weeds, diseases and insects that you find before trying to "manage" them. You may just be trying to do in a do-gooder!

The best way to identify an insect is to capture it and send the specimen to the university extension service. Some nurseries have excellent staff who know their insects, weeds and moulds, some have staff who don't. There are excellent field guides with colour photos of insects and weeds that also describe the habits of the species. An insect that looks, well, menacing, may just be helping your lawn to stay healthy. How do you know, unless you identify it and learn about it?

It is important to identify the "pest" to establish its friendliness to your other plants, because, in some cases, you may want to invite it to stay.

For example, clover in your lawn means that your soil is too dry and compacted for turf grass, but perfect for clover. Now, you can dig up or (gasp!) use a herbicide on the clover, but unless you remedy the problem with good maintenance practices such as aeration and amending the soil with organic fertilizers and compost to improve soil health and water retention, the clover will continue to win out over the grass.

But clover adds nitrogen to your soil naturally and needs less of our diminishing water supply to keep it healthy and green. It is soft, makes a great playing area for kids and animals, is low-growing so it needs no mowing and even sports pretty pinkish/purple or white blossoms once a year or so. So is it really a pest, or a guest? Do you want to encourage this zero maintenance ground-cover to take up permanent residence by doing, well, nothing, or fight it with labour, money, precious water and fertilizers?

## 7. When pests persist
Potion or practice?

Okay. You've read this book, talked the talk and walked the walk—and those pests are *still* a problem. Excellent cultural practices and maintenance procedures have made no difference. Now what?

Your plants are trying to tell you something. The grasses/vegetables/ornamentals having the pest problems simply will not do well in that spot in your yard, perhaps anywhere in your yard, because of incompatible soil and/or climate conditions.

So rather than mixing up "least toxic" organic potions to attack the pest (and some innocent bystanders) this time around, deal with the problem by moving or replacing the plants in question with ones that will thrive in that exact spot in your yard just the way it is. Plant grasses, vegetables and ornamentals that *like* your soil, sun, shade, drainage and climate. *That's* organic pest control.

These basic steps and the program outlined in the following chapters, will provide you with healthy soil and plants maintained in a way that respects and assists the balance of nature. Instead of very toxic chemicals and "least toxic potions" that don't solve the problems, instead of little signs that keep you and your kids off the grass and last-spray-date advisories for your vegetables, you will be growing plants in a way that discourages pests in the first place and in a way that welcomes you to join the birds, butterflies, ladybugs, earthworms and occasional dandelion in your organic yard. A colourful, song-filled, safe environment.

**3**

# HEALTHY SOIL, HEALTHY PLANTS

N o amount of healthy soil, no cultural practice, no least toxic remedy, or synthetic pesticide is going to keep a plant that doesn't belong in your garden or yard pest-free. It's that simple.

## SOIL
Laying the groundwork

Having said that, successful lawns, gardens and landscaping depend on healthy topsoil, the 20-cm (8-in.) layer of nutrient-rich earth which sustains plant life. Neglected or chemically abused soil usually suffers from some or all of the following maladies:

- poor air circulation, or compaction
- excessive or inadequate drainage
- inadequate or imbalanced nutrient content
- out-of-balance pH
- the absence of worms, bugs, bacteria and other soil life needed to break up the earth and make nutrients available for plants

It's really simple:

UNHEALTHY SOIL = STRESSED PLANTS

STRESSED PLANTS = PEST MAGNETS

So getting your soil into healthy shape is essential for a healthy yard.

This chapter outlines a program that will help you wean your soil from chemical dependency and maintain a nutritious and well balanced medium for your plants. Healthy soil breeds healthy plants. And healthy plants can fend off weeds, insects and diseases without chemical treatments.

## SOIL TESTING

It's a pretty good bet that your soil is generally nutrient deficient, especially if it has been abused with chemical fertilizers, insecticides, herbicides and fungicides, or neglected completely. It will likely need topping up with organic amendments to balance the pH and correct for deficiencies. Without these additions, your soil will continue to produce weak and vulnerable plants.

Before you start feeding the soil, *test it*! There are home kits for soil testing sold at nurseries that will tell you the pH (acidity/alkalinity) of your soil, as well as the amounts of nitrogen, phosphorus and

**Soil Thieves**

For those moving into newly built homes, a word of caution. Building contractors have been known to remove the top 15 cm (6 in.) of topsoil before you arrive, laying sod and planting out gardens on a thin inadequate layer of subsoil. You then have problems "built" right in. Make sure your contractor leaves a full 20 cm (8 in.) of topsoil at the site. Otherwise, it may be scraped off, sold to a local nursery and sold back to you.

potassium. The advantage of testing *before* you feed is that your results will tell you what your soil needs, so you won't be over-feeding or under-feeding with a particular nutrient. Proper amounts in feeding are important for your soil, plants and pest reduction strategy, because some pests are attracted to too much or too little of a nutrient in a plant.

You can also have a professional lab test your soil for nutrients. Labs will take more time to get you the results, but they will provide much more detailed information. If you can find a lab that provides organic results, they will give you exact quantities that your soil needs of each amendment to correct the pH and nutrient balance. (See **Resources**.)

Get your soil tested in the very early spring, to make sure you have the results back in time for feeding your ornamental flower and plant beds. (Lawns should be fed only once a year, in the fall.) You need only test every four to five years. Contact the lab beforehand for information about soil collection, shipping, fees and response times. An organic analysis can cost anywhere from $30 to $80. The first time, ask for results on levels of nitrogen, phosphorus, potassium, sculpture, calcium and magnesium, as well as pH.

**pH**

On a 14 point scale, pH of 7 is neutral, less than 7 is acid, greater than 7 is alkaline. The majority of cool weather grasses and plants enjoy a slightly acid pH of 6.5. However, some plants have special requirements for acidic soil (below pH 6.5) or more alkaline soil (above pH 7). For information about specific plants, check gardening reference books, or at the nursery where you shop.

# THE pH FACTOR
Sweet or sour?

Your soil needs to be the correct pH for the plants you are growing as acidity affects the availability of nutrients to your plants.

As soil drops below pH 6, phosphorus, potassium, calcium and magnesium will become less available to your plants. If your soil is above pH 7, iron will be less available to your plants. So proper pH has a lot to do with your plants getting the nutrients they need.

The following amendments are available for adjusting soil pH. Add only in the amounts recommended by your soil test results, as over-liming can seriously damage the pH of your soil.

- Dolomite lime (high magnesium) increases alkalinity where soil needs magnesium as well as calcium
- Hi-cal lime (high in calcium) increases alkalinity where soil has adequate or excessive magnesium
- Flowers of sulphur increases soil acidity.

Apply all lime or flowers of sulphur as required in fall or spring, well in advance of planting. Spread evenly and thoroughly and make sure to wear a protective mask or kerchief and gloves to prevent inhalation of these fine powders. Gently rake into the top inch of soil, water and let rest.

## ORGANIC FERTILIZERS
Feed a soil, starve a pest

Healthy soil contains a variety of nutrients that are gradually released into the soil as organic material decomposes. And you thought it was just "dirt."

The three main nutrients required for plant health are nitrogen, phosphorus and potassium. Blended fertilizers are usually identified according to their percentages of each of these three. For example, (21–7–7) fertilizer contains 21 percent nitrogen, 7 percent phosphorus and 7 percent potassium.

The following amendments are recommended for balancing the nutrients in your soil's diet. Add only in the amount recommended by your soil test results, as over-feeding can disrupt the soil's ecosystem and even attract pests. Do not exceed the annual maximum

**Nix Pre-mix**

Pre-mixed organic fertilizers are not the way to go. Your soil's needs are not likely to match the ratios of ingredients in the manufacturer's blend. Better to purchase and apply the particular nutrients that your soil requires, in the proper amounts as indicated by your soil test. This will ensure balanced feeding.

dose. In the listings, the bracketed numbers (2–2–2) stand for the percentage of nitrogen, phosphorus, and potassium, respectively contained in the nutrient source. Maximum application rates for each year are given, followed by the length of time the treatment should last.

In making the switch to organics, fall applications are best for established lawns and spring applications for gardens and new lawn beds. Make sure to apply at least six to eight weeks before planting. Mix the nutrients into the top 2.5cm (1 in.) of soil with a rake, water and let rest. If your lawn or plants are already established, apply as a top dressing, especially after aeration (see Chapter 4).

Cover your mouth and nose with a filtered mask to prevent inhalation of the powders. If you are mixing your nutrients before spreading, put on your mask and gloves first, then use a large dry container and a wooden spoon. Carry small quantities of the fertilizer in a quart pitcher, larger quantities in a wheelbarrow or spreader and apply as evenly as possible.

## CORN GLUTEN MEAL

There is a new product on the market that seems to be the perfect answer to weed and feed. The protein part of corn, corn gluten meal, is a milling byproduct. It not only inhibits root growth, it contains 10 percent nitrogen by weight, making it a fertilizer and herbicide. Because of its herbicidal properties, however, it falls into the "potion" category of organic pesticides. It will kill *any* emergent broad-leaved plant - it is not species specific and doesn't remedy the problem that brought the weed to your yard in the first place. For that reason I don't recommend it.

NOTE: There are many organic sources out there. I recommend the following as the least environmentally disruptive:

**Mow 'n' Feed**
If your soil in your lawn tests well, all you may need to do is leave the grass clippings on it each time you mow. Clippings provide great compost and are a good fertilizer in themselves, providing just the right amount of nitrogen. Talk about perfect recycling.

## ORGANIC NITROGEN SOURCES:

**Fish meal:** (10.5–6–0) Maximum 2.5 kg/10 m$^2$, or 5 lb./100 sq. ft.) lasts five months.

**Blood meal**: (12.5–1–3) Maximum 1.5 kg/10 m$^2$, or 3 lb./100 sq. ft.) lasts four months.

**Feather Meal**: (12–1–0) Apply according to label instructions.

## ORGANIC PHOSPHOROUS SOURCES:

**Bone meal**: (3–20–0) plus 20-30 percent calcium. Maximum 2.5 kg/10 m$^2$ or 5 lb./100 sq.ft. Lasts more than 12 months.

**Single super phosphate**: (0–20–0) plus 20 percent calcium and 12 percent sulphur. Maximum 2.5 kg/10 m$^2$ or 5 lb./100 sq. ft. Starts release in 2-3 months.

**Fish bone meal**: (4–22–0) May attract animals

## ORGANIC POTASSIUM SOURCES

**Kelp meal and liquid seaweed**: (1–0–1.2) plus 23 percent trace minerals. Maximum 0.5 kg/10 m$^2$ or 1 lb./100 sq. ft. Lasts 6-12 months

**Wood Ash**: (0–0–1) to (0–0–10) Variable nutrient levels. Ashes of hardwood sare the best and raise soil pH too. Maximum 1 kg/10m$^2$ or 2 lb./100 sq. ft. Last 12+ months.

**Sulphate of potash magnesia (sulpomag)**: (0–0–22) plus 11 percent magnesium and 22 percent sulphur. Use where calcium is plentiful and magnesium and potassium are deficient.

**Sulphate of potash**: (0–0–50) plus 18 percent sulphur. Use where potassium is deficient.

**K-Mag (langbeinite)**: (0–0–22) Soluble source of sulphur, potash, magnesium.

## OTHER NATURAL SUPPLEMENTS

**Seaweed:** as much as you can, any time, just as it is, as a side-dressing on veggies, fruits and ornamentals. Don't rinse it first. There are valuable minerals in the salty coating and it won't hurt your plants.

**Calcium Sulphate:** 23-57 percent calcium, 17 percent sulphur. Use where magnesium needs to be reduced and calcium added, but where pH levels are already adequate or even on the high side. Use only according to test results, from 0.5-5 kg/10 $m^2$ or from 1-10 lb./100 sq. ft.

**Leonardite and other mixtures:** approximately 15 percent humic materials and 15 percent humic acid. A source of concentrated humates that help make nutrients available to plants. Apply in fall, or a month before compost is added.

### The Rock Phosphate Debate

The phosphate in single super phosphate is not radioactive, unlike the rock phosphates originating in North American mine sites, which have high uranium content. That's why North American rock phosphates are not recommended here. Greensand, a potassium source, is also high in uranium and so has also been left off the list.

## COMPOST
That old black magic

All soils benefit from nutrient-rich applications of compost, all the time, any time. Lawn soils, too. So compost, compost, compost. Made from rotted organic matter, compost is the best all-around soil conditioner available, period. It improves the physical and biological condition of your soil by providing beneficial microorganisms, excellent drainage and both major and minor plant nutrients. It can be added to your soil throughout the season. It's impossible to use too much.

Some municipalities are even getting into the act, picking up organic matter with other recyclables at doorsteps and manufacturing their own compost, available free or at low cost. Many have made composting bins available at discounted prices, along with starter kits and information packages.

# HOW TO MAKE IT
Let it rot

Commercial compost mixes are available in garden supply centres, but making your own is inexpensive and easy. It also helps to reduce the volume of waste going to municipal dumpsites.

Keep a pair of sharp scissors, designated for the purpose, near the kitchen compost container. This can be a small bowl, or bucket with a lid. Then simply cut kitchen vegetable waste (fruit and vegetable peelings) and add to non-meat leftovers, coffee grounds, egg-shells, etc. The smaller the better, in terms of instant compost gratification.

If you are close to a real live seaweed source, put it in your compost pile for the best booster ever, just as it is. *Don't rinse seaweed; it just takes off all the wonderful minerals.*

When the container begins to bug you, take it outside and dump it into your compost bin, along with any fallen leaves the neighbours have been silly enough to rake up for garbage removal, excess grass clippings, some seaweed if you have access to it and the occasional sprinkle of sand. Turn the pile over every few days—and voila!

Avoid meat or bones as they will attract vermin. Ditto oily foods such as butter, cooking oils, etc., as they will smother the bacteria in the bin and slow down the rotting process.

Large amounts of compost can be prepared inoffensively in a compost container or bin. If you are using an open container, locate it in a sunny spot at the edge of your garden, exposed to air on all sides. You can use a perforated garbage can, cylinders made from chicken wire or snow fencing, or a four-foot square stacked cement block bin, open on one side for easy access.

Many municipalities are subsidizing the purchase of open and closed bins made from recycled plastic. The closed bins are smaller and require less work from you.

It's simply a matter of adding matter and, in the best of the bins, pulling out a drawer at the bottom several weeks later that is filled with perfect compost.

A recipe for dynamite compost follows. The end product is ready to use when it is cool, dark and crumbly. It's okay if some shape of the original organic matter is evident.

## THE 14-DAY COMPOST RECIPE

This is for the eager compost beaver, who is willing to put in some work for a fairly quick reward. This pile can be composted in two weeks in hot weather, or under a thermal blanket of snow, if the materials are shredded. Use a power shredder, or cut small as you go in the kitchen:

- 3,700 cm$^2$ (4 sq. ft.) compost bin, open on on side

- 2.5 cm (1 in.) base layer of brush on bottom, such as grass clippings, ruined hay or straw

- 15 cm (6 in.) of "green matter"such as kitchen peels, eggshells, coffee grounds, ruined hay or leaves

- 5 cm (2 in.) of sterilized manure

- a sprinkling of topsoil and limestone

Repeat the layers until the pile reaches at least 1 m (3 ft.) high. Using a pitchfork, turn and moisten the pile on the fourth, seventh and 10th days, after at least a cubic metre (or cubic yard) of material has been collected and shredded. Presto! Black magic.

## ROTTED MANURE
True recycling

Rotted or composted manure is another balanced source of available nutrients for your soil. Manure is widely available in bags for home use in supermarkets and garden centres. Make sure it is sterilized, so that any weed seeds have been killed. If you buy manure "fresh off the farm," there is always the chance that it has not been adequately rotted and that it will introduce weeds into your lawn and garden. If a farm is your only source, try to get the manure without "bedding" in it.

Lay on about 50 kg/10 m$^2$ or 100 pounds/100 sq. ft. in your garden early each spring, six weeks before planting. Rake it into the top 2.5 cm (1 in.) of soil, water and let sit.

## BUYING TOPSOIL
Panacea or pain?

General wisdom has it that we should avoid buying topsoil at all costs. There are several reasons for this. One is that we may be buying weeds, insects and diseases along with the soil. If the soil you are buying has been declared "weed, insects and disease free" make sure that it has been "manufactured" from scratch and not hijacked from another area, private or public. A better idea is to create your own topsoil, by composting, adding sand available at your local nursery and extremely well-rotted, weed-free manure.

### Build a Bin

Compost bins can be easily constructed in your yard with very little effort or expense.

A perforated garbage can, a chicken-wire circle, or a three-sided stacked brick structure (see opposite page) is all you need. Locate the bins at the edge of the garden, in full sun to speed breakdown.

To eliminate odours and accelerate decomposition inside open bins, add sand or soil every week and stir regularly to add oxygen.

You can use a pitch-fork for large piles or a compost stirrer available at most nurseries for smaller enclosures. When the pile has shrunk in size, you know it's working.

## TO DIG OR NOT TO DIG?

That is the question

In the years since the first edition of this book came out, much information has surfaced about the vast communities of beneficial organisms in soil and how digging can disrupt them. Where we were once advised to "double dig" vegetable beds for French intensive gardening, the wisdom of this day is to lay the shovels down and add compost, fertilizers and other supplements on top of the soil, allowing the nutrients to soak in naturally.

However, if you are not about to plant a tree in the garden, some digging is necessary, obviously.

So, new rules and common sense: *Don't* dig in any soil additives (manure, compost, organic fertilizers) beyond a light raking. *Do* dig soil to prepare for large root masses, disturbing the surrounding soil as little as possible. If your soil has become compacted over the winter, aeration and addition of compost is the answer to friable soil for this season.

Ready to select plants!

# THE CHEMICAL-FREE LAWN

## 4

*T*his chapter tells you how to select, plant, water, mow, feed, aerate and generally maintain your lawn without chemical fertilizers and pestcides. If you follow these basic steps, you will have a healthy lawn that optimizes growth of grasses and minimizes opportunities for pest insect, weeds, or diseases.

A word about lawn-care and landscaping contractors: a survey completed in several North American cities showed that customers are *still* unaware that chemical pesticides are routinely used on their premises. Ask your lawn care contractor exactly what he or she uses on your yard. Advocate a switch to the pesticide-free regimen outlined in this book and if the contractor is reluctant, shop elsewhere.

## SELECTING NEW GRASSES OR UPGRADING OLD TURF

To minimize maintenance requirements, pests and diseases, it is essential that you start by choosing grass varieties that are pest resistant and well adapted to your climate and soil. If you try to grow a grass that does not like your soil or climate, you will not succeed. It's that simple. So take a look at the map below dividing the warm and cool grass-growing regions and look at the varieties mentioned very carefully for your region. Spend a little more on higher-end (more pest-resistant) grasses and you'll save thousands of dollars on remedies and replacement.

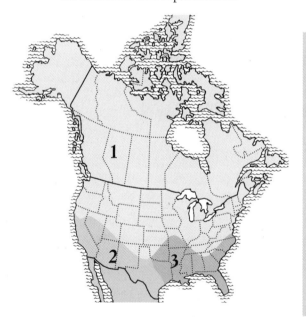

**1. COOL-SEASON GRASSES:**
Kentucky blues
Tall fescues
Perennial ryes
Buffalo
Blue grama

**2. WARM GRASSES WEST:**
Bermuda
Zoysia

**3. WARM GRASSES EAST:**
Bahia
St. Augustine
Centipede
Zoysia
Bermuda

Within each region, there are vast differences in soil and climate. Select grasses and plants that suit each area of your yard.

A description of each of the cool and warm season grasses follows, along with a list of recommended cultivars for each. Remember, you want the best, so ask for it and don't plant/sod/plug/overseed until you get it. This will save countless hours and dollars down the road.

## THE COOL SEASON GRASSES

If you are starting a new lawn, prepare your soil according to your test results and the requirements of the grasses you select. The rule of thumb for cool season grasses is: Blend! To optimize pest resistance, drought resistance, just-about-anything-resistance, three grass species are better than one. This is because while one in the blend is languishing in that punishing drought, the other two, more drought-resistant, will still look fairly good. Diversity promotes strength. And lawns need as much diversity as they can get.

I know, everyone wants a carpet of that gorgeous Kentucky bluegrass. But if you plant it by itself, you are asking for problems. Actually, you are asking every Kentucky blue-loving problem in the region to dinner. So diversify as much as possible.

Seed with a mix of perennial ryegrasses, annual ryegrasses (to germinate quickly and fill in the spaces before the weeds can), tall fescues and Kentucky blues. Water generously, keep moist in the daytime only and prevent foot traffic.

If your lawn—composed of who-knows-what—is already in place, aerate it three times the first year in spring, summer and fall and then overseed with one each of the high-end tall fescues, perennial ryes and Kentucky bluegrasses listed below to upgrade your turf.

When you buy sod, try to find a sod that has a blend of the listed cultivars built right in. If your supplier doesn't have a blend, look elsewhere, or ask that it be grown and wait a season.

Look for good root development on sod and make sure your topsoil is deep and healthy before you plant.

And *do* spend the extra dollars to get the very best seed/turf available. The recommended varieties, below, have

### Moss is Boss

Just as attempts to grow any kind of turf grass in the desert are silly, so too is trying to force turf to out-compete mosses in the Pacific Northwest yard and other damp, dark climes. Give it up and learn to love your moss: it's soft, green, needs no mowing, fertilizer or water and will win out over turf grass in those cool wet spots no matter what you do.

all tested high for heat/drought/cold/insect/weed/disease tolerance, as well as for green-up, density, etc.

Many are not yet available to the home consumer (they are still reserved for golf courses and other professional users) because there is an assumption that you won't want to spend the extra money to get the best cultivars. That's why when you buy grass seed at most outlets now, the cultivars aren't even listed by name. The bag will say so much Kentucky blue, so much perennial rye, etc. The problem with that system is that there are hundreds of Kentucky blue, perennial rye and tall fescue cultivars to choose from. If your bag doesn't name the cultivars, you are buying no-name, generic, cheap grasses that are not very pest or climate resistant.

This is unacceptable. Begin to educate your nursery staff and through them, their suppliers and through them, the seed producers—that you want only the best, because

## Establish Reasonable Tolerance Levels
### Pesticides are toxic, buttercups aren't

It is important to remember that all lawns harbour some "pests," whether or not pesticides are used. The trick is to keep the numbers low enough to prevent significant damage to the grass plants. What constitutes significant damage and more important, what constitutes a healthy lawn, is a very personal decision.

If you want a perfect green carpet, buy one and nail it down. Otherwise, you should be prepared to enjoy a few buttercups or primroses.

Very few weeds or insects actually harm your lawn. Some weeds, such as creeping Charlie and buttercups, are quite attractive. Others are beneficial to your soil. Clover provides grass plants with nitrogen.

Take some time to think about your priorities. Putting-green, zero-weed tolerance, lots of toxic chemicals? Or playground for your children and pets, zero chemicals and some buttercups? Hmm...

the best means fewer dollars on remedies and replacement. Where grasses are concerned, you really do get what you pay for. And as money talks, more of the best cultivars will soon be readily available, much as organic fertilizers are now, after a decade of consumer demand.

In general, perennial ryegrasses don't live as long a Kentucky blues, so you'll have to overseed with it to keep a diverse mix. Add at least once a year after aeration.

Some of the ryegrasses listed below have naturally occurring endophytes, a fungus that resists diseases and some common lawn insects like sod webworms and armyworms. Cool! Ask you nursery about their availability.

## COOL-SEASON TURF CHARACTERISTICS

**Kentucky bluegrass** is dark green, has a medium leaf texture and forms a dense, beautiful lawn, making it a favourite. It has medium drought resistance and medium heat resistance. Kentucky blue likes the sun and does poorly in shady areas. It recovers quickly from occasional traffic, but is not considered "tough." Kentucky blue likes moderate water and performs best in rich, fertile soil, low in acid, with good drainage. When fed too much nitrogen, this grass will develop thatch and is more prone to diseases, weeds and insects than the ryegrasses or fescues. For this reason it is a good idea to blend Kentucky blue with other types of cool-season grasses for a diverse, healthy lawn.

**Perennial ryegrass** has a moderately dark green leaf, fine in texture and quick to sprout. It has good density and produces attractive, tough leaves. It has excellent heat and cold tolerance and good drought tolerance. It will go dormant during a short drought, but will recover with the first water. This grass shows moderate tolerance to filtered shade and wears well in moderate foot traffic and recreation areas.

It has moderate water needs and produces no thatch, as the grass reproduces by tillers instead of stolons or rhizomes. It is highly adaptable to a wide range of soils, from light and sandy, to heavy and clayey. It has excellent resistance to diseases and insects and as long as overseeding is carried out on a regular basis, weeds should not be a problem.

**Tall fescues** are medium to dark green in colour and have a more extensive root system than any other cool season turf grass. It is excellent for transition zones, those areas close to the line between cool and warm season regions on the map. Its strong wearability makes it an excellent choice for residential recreation areas. Tall fescues have good heat tolerance for a cool season grass, but are less cold-resistant.

Because it has such a deep root system, it is an excellent grass in periods of drought. It prefers full sun, but is moderately tolerant of partial shade. Tall fescues need moderate amounts of water and form very little thatch. These grasses adapt to a wide range of soil conditions and have many varieties that are resistant to diseases and insects. To control weeds, make sure your turf is dense.

## BEST COOL-SEASON GRASSES

All of the following grasses are known for their hardiness and all have tested high for turf quality and resistance to many diseases and insects. All do well in cool-season climates. These are the cream of the crop and are still hard to find in store-bought mixes produced for residential use. Whine, complain and generally make a nuisance of yourself until these cultivars become available for the home-owner. Remember, most of these are already available to specialty

| Best Kentucky blues | Best perennial ryegrasses | Best tall fescues |
| --- | --- | --- |
| Bartita | Roberts-627 | Kitty Hawk |
| Dragon | PST 2BR | Apache II |
| Eagleton | Applaud | Renegade |
| Baronie | Pennington 11301 | Olympic Gold |
| Kenblue | Amazing (B1) | Rembrandt |
| South Dakota | Pizazz | Wolfpack |
| | All Star 2 | Rebel 2000 |
| | Calypso II | Plantation |
| | Kokomo | (Pennington 1901) |

turf users, so start to include yourself on that elite list and get your nursery to order—*by name*—one of each of the above from their suppliers, then blend and spread.

A good, basic mix would be 30 percent Kentucky blue, 30 percent perennial rye, 40 percent tall fescue.

## THE WARM-SEASON GRASSES

Warm season grasses like it hot. Actually they like it long and hot—long summers where temperatures are consistently over 30° C (85° F). Warm season grasses do most of their growing in summer. Because they turn brown in winter, it's a good idea to overseed lawns made of these grasses with some cool season grasses in early fall, such as ryegrasses and fescue. This will help you to have a green lawn year-round. (See map, page 44.)

Warm season grasses are unfortunately prone to weeds and thatch. Dethatch and overseed to prevent these problems. The stems of the warm season grasses are so strong and wiry, that, for the most part, you will need a reel mower to handle cutting jobs.

## WARM-SEASON GRASS CHARACTERISTICS

**Bahia grass** is a tough, coarse grass that roots very deeply and extensively, making it an excellent choice for areas that are prone to erosion. It has excellent shade and drought tolerance, is low-growing and resistant to thatch. It is considered high-maintenance, however, because you will need to mow it frequently with a sharp rotary mower.

This grass likes sandy, poorly fertile soils and stays green into the cool winter months. Some diseases and insects are a problem with Bahia grass.

Bahia grass comes in sod or seed and likes full sun or partial shade. This grass is a great choice for the southern coastal plains of the United States.

**Bermuda grass** has two types: common Bermuda and hybrid or "improved" Bermuda. Common Bermuda produces seeds that blow and set with abandon—often on to your neighbour's lawn. It is also more susceptible to diseases and insects.

Go hybrid. The hybrids are softer, denser, greener and more finely textured. Hybrids are heat-loving, drought-tolerant and very durable, making an excellent choice for lawns with high traffic. They actually like it up to 43° C (110° F). Like all warm-season grasses, they do not like the shade. You can overseed with perennial ryes and tall fescues in the winter to maintain a green lawn all year 'round.

Bermuda grasses like moderate water and are well adapted to infertile, well-drained sandy soil. They like pH of 5 to 6.5. Hybrid Bermudas come in sod and sprigs. Plant sprigs at a rate of 80$l$/100 m$^2$ (2 bu./1,000 sq. ft.) or 5-cm (2-in.) plugs 30 cm (12 in.) apart. Plant in full sun.

**Centipede grass** is medium to light green, with a medium- to fine-textured grass blade. It likes hot humid tropical climates and grows well in areas of high rainfall. Another heat lover, centipede grass likes temperatures up to 38° C (100° F) and tends to go dormant in temperatures below 13° C (55° F).

It's a very low-maintenance grass. It has moderate drought resistance and adapts well to shade. It does not like heavy traffic and will recover slowly from heavy wear.

Because it is slow-growing, centipede grass requires less mowing. It produces little thatch, usually out-competes weeds and is fairly disease- and insect-free.

Centipede grass prefers acidic soil and is well adapted to infertile, well-drained soil, but doesn't like sea spray and is one of the first grasses to go dormant (brown) in hot weather.

Centipede grass comes in sod, seed and 5 cm (2 in.) sprigs. Plant sprigs 200-240$l$/100 m$^2$ (5-6 bushels/1,000 sq. ft.); plugs 15-23 cm (6-9 in.) apart. Seed at 0.5-1 kg/100 m$^2$ (1-2 lb./1,000 sq. ft.) Plant in full sun or moderate shade.

**St. Augustine grass** is a very fast-growing, deep-rooted grass of medium to dark green colour. It has coarse-to medium-textured blades and reproduces by sending out stolons along the soil surface. St. Augustine is an excellent grass for coastal regions with hot, tropical climates. It thrives in heat and is salt hardy. St. Augustine grass likes temperatures up to 40° C (105° F) and will go dormant when temperatures drop below 13° C (55° F).

There is a wide range in drought tolerance depending on the variety of St. Augustine grass used. Different varieties also show a wide range in adaptation to shade.

It is susceptible to thatch and to the resultant pests if thatch is ignored, as well as a virus called St. Augustine Decline (SAD). Look for resistant varieties.

Its water needs are moderate to high: St. Augustine grass thrives on wet yards, so make sure you have plenty of rainfall before you choose this grass. If you mow your lawn lower than 5-8 cm (2-3 in.) you'll thin out the St. Augustine grass and the weeds will move in. Mow high, mow reel.

It grows a wide range of soils, but likes neutral to alkaline soils the best. As with all grasses, a well-maintained lawn will provide the best weed control. Some varieties are resistant to chinch bugs and the SAD virus.

St. Augustine grass comes in sod or plugs, which should be planted 30 cm (1ft.) apart in full sun to moderate shade.

**Zoysia** grass ranges in colour from medium to dark green and forms a dense, low-maintenance lawn. It grows slowly and so takes time to fill in after planting, but is very easy to maintain once it has filled in. Zoysia is a wiry grass that likes hot, humid, tropical climates and can withstand very heavy traffic. It tolerates heat up to 38° C (100° F) and turns dormant below 13° C (55° F).

Zoysia has moderate to good drought resistance and takes heat as well as any other grass. It is also well adapted to growing in the shade and has the best wear resistance of any warm season grass.

Zoysia needs very little water, which is excellent in these days of water scarcity. Water deeply and infrequently, making sure your lawn stays thick to prevent weed germination and growth. This is the only grass that really likes to be kept short: mow 2.5-5 cm (1-2 in.) high. Take it very easy on the nitrogen or thatch will form.

Zoysia grass is excellent in salty, infertile soil. Some varieties have excellent resistance to diseases and insects. Because it is such a dense turf, weeds are usually not a problem.

Zoysia grass comes in 5-cm (2-in.) plugs or sod. Plant plugs 15 cm (6 in.) apart in full sun or partial shade.

## BEST WARM-SEASON GRASSES

These have been rated for overall turf quality, diseases such as brown patch, rust, yellow patch, leaf spot, insects such as zoysia mite, mole cricket, chinch bug, as well as for drought tolerance, colour, green-up and density, etc. by the National Turfgrass Evaluation Program in the United States. (See **Resources**)

| **Best Bermuda hybrids** | **Best St. Augustines** | **Best zoysia** |
|---|---|---|
| Blackjack | Delmar | De Anza |
| Blue-Muda | Floratam | El Toro |
| Princess | Floritine | Emerald |
| Riviera | Raleigh | Jamur |
| Shanghai | Seville | Meyer |
| Tifgreen | | Zorro |
| Tiflawn | | |

Centipede and Bahia grasses have not been rated by the NTEP, but I have listed a few of each that have the best reputations:

**Centipede grass**
Centiseed (only available as seed)
Oaklawn (available in sprig)

**Bahia grass:**
Argentine
Paraguay
Pensacola

## HOW TO PLANT

Lay your new sod, plug or seed according to density indicated on the label, factoring in the percentage of the other members of your new blend. Then after seeding or sodding, roll lightly, water, keep moist and protected until the grass has grown in. Make sure you plant a blend in cool-season regions and overseed with quick-growing ryes and fescues to fill in the area quickly, out-competing weeds.

## A WORD ABOUT NATIVE LAWNS: YES!

**Buffalo grass:** In the Great Plains of North America—that huge area from central Alberta east to central Manitoba, south to encompass most of south Texas—Buffalo grass, (*Buchloe dactyloides*) makes an excellent lawn replacement.

It has lived on the plains for centuries, evolving efficient water use and sod-forming ability. And once it has filled in and been mowed, it looks like a beautiful "real" lawn. It is sage green in colour, fine bladed, does well in full sun or partial shade and has very low water requirements. After the first year, it should need no water at all, although to keep it green in drought conditions, you could use a drip hose once a month.

It only grows to 12.5 cm (5 in.), so it needs mowing only every few weeks. It doesn't need or even *like* fertilizer and does not produce thatch or have insect pests. And it attracts native birds to your yard.

**Blue grama** grass (*Bouteloua gracilis*) grows well on the plains and even into California. It's another great turfgrass lawn replacement. The lawn at the Santa Barbara Botanic Garden is blue grama, and looks just like a "real" lawn. It's a perennial, with blue-green colour, likes full sun and very low water, will grow in dry, poor soils and can be planted from seeds or seedlings. No fertilizer, no thatch, no insects. Mowed, it looks like a very conventional yard and after its first season will need no watering.

For photos and more information on these two grasses and other great native possibilities, see *How to get Your Lawn Off Grass* (C. Rubin) under **Further Reading**.

## MAINTENANCE
### An ounce of prevention

Some of the folks who study lawn grass for a living estimate that 80-90 percent of pest problems can be avoided by proper lawn and soil care. Take care of your yard and prevent pest problems in the first place. There are five basic maintenance steps that *must* be followed to build a pest-resistant lawn:

## 1. Aeration
### The breath of life

A major cause of weed problems in North America is compaction of the soil immediately around and under the roots of your grass plants.

**Buyer Beware**

Beware of the "aerators" that punch depressions into the sod, like nails, spikes, or those "aerator sandals" that have spiked soles. They actually compact the soil even more, directly around the hole.

Most grass cultivars have very fine, hair-like roots. And compaction is exactly what it sounds like: the particles of your soil have been squeezed tightly together, preventing nutrients, water and oxygen from reaching the roots. The result? Roots are stressed, plants are stressed, they begin to die out and opportunistic weeds with roots from hell move in.

The remedy? Aeration!

There are hand and power-driven tools that cut and lift narrow plugs out of your yard, allowing oxygen and amendments to penetrate the soil and restoring proper drainage.

Most lawns should be aerated at least twice a year, once in early spring and once in the fall. This timetable avoids periods when problem weeds are germinating.

After spring aeration, top-dress with screened compost and pest-resistant grass varieties listed above and lime or sulphur as needed. Immediately after aerating in fall, top-dress, (spread) with compost and fertilize as needed using the amendments suggested in Chapter 2.

If this is your first year "going organic," aerate three to four times per year, as your soil will certainly be compacted. Midseason aeration is recommended for lawns with heavy thatch and for top-dressing sod with compost and pest-resistant ryegrasses.

After spring aeration, spread compost and a blend of pest-resistant, high-end grass seed over your lawn. Use the back of a rake to gently force the mixture into the holes made by aeration, then water and let rest. In mid-summer, aerate again, adding more compost and seeds, especially if this is your first season "going organic."
In fall, aerate, add compost and fertilize according to test soil results, with the recommended organic amendments.

You may want to get together with your neighbours and purchase or rent an aerating tool or machine. Have a neighbourhood party. Hand-held, self-propelled, towable and tractor-mounted models are available. Check with your local garden supply or rental centre. Be careful—avoid underground cables.

## 2. Dispatch that thatch

There is a great debate going on across North America about "thatch." So here's the poop, so to speak:

- Thatch is a dense layer of undecomposed plant matter compacted on the surface of your soil in a greyish brown, fibrous mat. It has the appearance and consistency of a coconut fibre doormat.

- Thatch is caused by a combination of factors including decreased soil microbial activity, too much fertilizer, poor aeration and drainage and pesticide use—particularly fungicides which reduce microbial activity.

- Thatch resists decay.

- A thick layer of thatch will prevent water from soaking into the soil beneath. Thus, the tops or "crowns" of the grasses remain wet, while the roots are too dry. This produces all kinds of problems. When the roots of your grass plants receive less water than they need and the soil surface retains too much, both roots and blades provide perfect breeding grounds for plant diseases and insects. (See illustration opposite.)

- Thatch increases your lawns susceptibility to cold, heat and drought.

Thatch is *not* the very healthy and beneficial layer of natural mulch at the base of your grass plants. As your grass clippings and other vegetative material decompose, a moist and easily penetrated mulch will be created, green, yellow or dark brown in colour. It's easy to poke a hole in this natural mulch with your finger. This stuff is good for your lawn —leave it there!

If you part your grass plants and find a dense fibrous mat that is hard, grey, more than 0.6 cm (¼ in.) thick and not porous, this is a message that you need to remove the thatch and improve your lawn maintenance.

If you discover thatch in late spring or summer, do not dethatch. Aerate your lawn as an interim measure and top-dress with screened compost.

Wait until the fall and dethatch with a thatch rake, made expressly for the purpose, or with a good vertical mower. Dethatching creates stress for your lawn, but it is temporary. Spring dethatching is not reommended. You can diminish the shock to your grass plants by top-dressing with compost and watering deeply and gently immediately after the fall procedure.

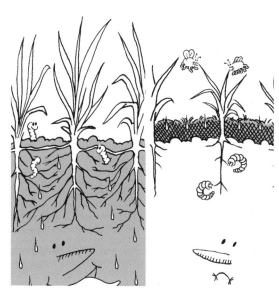

## 3. Food: It is what it eats

You already know about pH balance, organic fertilizers and compost from reading Chapter 2. This is just a reminder to apply that knowledge—and the goods—to your lawn to ensure a proper nutrient balance.

Fertilize established cool-season grasses in the fall. This will keep them growing longer into the winter and provide the plants with enough reserves in their stems and roots for quick green up in the spring. Contrary to popular belief, it is a very bad idea to feed cool-season grasses in the spring. You end up with blades that are too weak from too much food too early in the season and hungry roots. The biology of cool-season grasses informs us that they like to be fed just before going dormant, to feed the roots over the winter and store the excess food for the new spring shoots.

Warm-season grasses like to be fed from late spring to early fall. And when I say late spring, I mean late. The reason for this is to avoid giving any food to cool-season weeds. And if you fertilized too late in the fall, you'll be depriving your grass plants of the food they need to keep them strong during the cold weather.

Do not feed native grasses.

For cool-and warm-season grasses, add pH balancers in the spring, after aerating. Fertilize soil beds for new lawns during spring preparation. Add compost throughout the season by top-dressing after aeration.

## 4. Wise watering

Improper watering is one of the major causes of disease and insect problems in Canada and the United States. Each summer, neighbours watch neighbours watering their lawns through the afternoon and evening, moving sprinklers to a new spot every 20 minutes to half an hour. Bad boys and girls—this does way more harm than good.

Frequent shallow watering promotes shallow roots, which reduces the ability of the lawn to resist stress. Water long enough to allow a deep soaking to the roots, usually about one hour. One way to test how deep the water is going, is to set out an empty cup or glass dug in to soil level, so that water from your drip hose flows into it. When the water level in the glass reaches a depth of 2.5 cm (1 in.), it is time to move the hoses.

Soaker hoses are best in order to cut down on evaporation of our precious water. If your lawn is large, establish a watering rotation schedule, soaking a section each day.

When you water, use common sense: *do* use drip or soaker hoses. *don't* use "sprinklers." *do not* water in the evening: the sod will remain wet throughout the cool night,

## Water, Water, Everywhere—Not.

In periods of severe heat and drought, *let your lawn go dormant*. It will turn brown and some plants may suffer, but your lawn will not die. With the first fall rain, or watering, the plants will green up immediately. Another option is to install a gutter/rain barrel system to collect rainwater that can be applied to your lawn in periods of drought. Make sure the collection system is "closed" except for a spigot, to prevent mosquito breeding. Or use grey water, after it has washed your dishes or clothes. Or plant some of the many gorgeous native ground covers from your region that will only need water their first season to get established.

A lawn if you live in the desert? Unless you use *only* grey water, forget about it. There isn't enough drinking water to support such a silly whim—even in Canada and the United States. Desert states are actually paying citizens to replace their water-guzzling lawns and landscape with native plants. See *How to Get Your Lawn Off Grass*, C. Rubin, (**Further Reading**)

promoting fungus and disease. *Do not* water in the full hot summer sun: the water will evaporate and the sun will burn the grass. *Do* water in the early morning. This allows proper soaking before the burning sun or night chill sets in.

Allow your soil to become nearly dry between watering. For most lawns this means watering once every 10 days. Dry soil around grass plant roots inhibits weed seed germination and kills weed seedlings.

If puddles appear on your lawn after watering, part those grass plants and take a look. You may have a mat of thatch keeping water on the surface. If you can see no thatch, use a screwdriver or fork and probe the soil. If it is very compacted and hard to penetrate, you need to aerate and top-dress with screened compost to improve drainage. If puddles are appearing because your sod is uneven, level it by rolling up the turf, raking the topsoil level and replacing the turf. This will reduce waterlogged low spots that promote weeds and diseases.

Mowing too short, too often, is an invitation to weeds and disease

## 5. Mowing: The brush cut is dead

Mowing your lawn may seem an obvious procedure, but it's astonishing how many disease and weed problems are directly caused by improper mowing practices. Most lawns are mowed too short, too often. If frequent and close mowing is combined with other stresses such as drought, insufficient nutrients or cold spells, grass plants become smaller in size and less dense, providing perfect openings for opportunistic weeds.

Continual cutting also creates wounds at the end of grass blades, providing ports of entry for diseases such as leaf spot, rust and dollar spot. In fact, at the US Department of Agriculture's experimental lawn plots, it is standard practice to mow shorter and more often to encourage lawn diseases to move in, so they can be studied.

For cool season grasses, keep your blades sharp and as high off the ground as possible. In the spring and fall, when most grasses are in growing spurts, set the blade at 6.5-7.5 cm (2½-3 in.). In the summer months, set the blades at 7.5 cm (3 in.) for most varieties, or 10 cm (4 in.) if your lawn contains Canada bluegrass. Warm season grasses generally like to be cut much shorter.

Allow your grass to grow at least 2.5 cm (1 in.) above the mowing height before cutting it again. In general, cut once every 7-10 days. This gives grass time to recover from the previous mowing and to produce new blades of grass from the growing points. At the same time, it is sufficiently frequent to exhaust weed plants attempting to establish a home in your lawn.

Leave your grass clippings on your lawn! This is the best natural compost you can provide your grass plants. In fact, once your soil is aerated and nutritionally balanced, in future seasons you may only need your grass clippings as fertilizer.

In order to avoid compaction of the soil under your lawn, change your mowing patterns and points of entry to the lawn as often as possible. And if your cuttings are diseased, don't add them to your compost pile, or allow them to decompose on your lawn. Remove them and, if allowed, burn them.

### The Rule of Threes

Whether warm season or cool, whether cutting high or short, only remove one third of your grass blade during mowing. Cutting more than one-third of the blade at any time will weaken your plants, leaving them susceptible to weeds, insects and diseases. This is known as the Rule of Threes.

A word about mowers: if it uses gas and oil, make a sculpture out of it. A 3.5-horsepower lawn mower pollutes the air in a single mowing with as much exhaust as a new full-size car driven 560 kilometres (350 miles). The 50 million lawn mowers in the United States alone burn at least 1.13 billion litres (300 million US gallons) of gas per year. Seventy-six million litres (20 million gallons) of gasoline and oil are *spilled* each year in the United States, just refuelling lawn-care equipment. That's more than the Exxon Valdez spilled into the Gulf of Alaska in 1989. And electric mowers, while cleaner, use power. Mow high, mow sharp, mow manually.

## TIPS FOR TRANSITION
How to get your lawn off drugs

If your lawn is currently managed with chemical fertilizers and pesticides, it will need to go through a period of adjustment. To help build the soil and wean the plants from the chemical damage that has been done, aerate three times a year, in early spring, midsummer and fall and top-dress with pest-resistant seed and compost. Bag the clippings from the first few mowings, as the pesticide residue will prevent them from breaking down.

Next season, go ahead with the regular maintenance program. Aerate in spring and fall, and leave grass clippings on the ground.

If your lawn is recent sod, aerate in spring and at least twice in summer. Top-dress immediately afterward with coarse sand that most closely matches the size of your soil granules (available at your nursery) and compost. Aerate again in fall and add fertilizers and pH balancers. Of course, the previous steps should be followed throughout the season to minimize weed, disease and pest problems.

For those who "hire out": Give a copy of this book to your landscaping contractor to insure a shared understanding about your new lawn maintenance program.

**Transition Tip:**
One way to help build topsoil under the sod is to aerate three times a year and top-dress with screened compost, pest-resistant grass seed and coarse sand. Make sure the sand granules match your topsoil in size to avoid stratification.

A word of warning: if you simply leave your lawn on its own to go "cold turkey" from chemical treatment without extra help, it may not survive.

# MONITORING FOR INSECTS
Pest or Guest?

Every 10 days, just before you mow, randomly pick out four lawn sites to observe. The sites can be 30-90 cm (1-3 ft.) square, depending on the size of your lawn. Try to make sure that one of the areas is next to a sidewalk, patio or building.

Carefully examine each site for signs of pest problems, such as circular yellow or brown spots, bare spots, or slow or unusual growth. If any one insect seems particularly abundant, count the number in the given area and collect a sample for identification. This may be the culprit. Take the sample for identification to the public library university extension service, or ask the staff at your local garden centre.

Choose one or two of your monitoring sites (particularly one with dying grass and no visible cause). Cut three sides of a 30-cm (1 ft.) square in the sod at the edge of the damaged area and take a peek underneath. Look for grubs or other pests feeding on your roots. Count the numbers of each and collect specimens for identification. One root feeder poses no immediate threat, but some species are dangerous in low numbers.

Alternatively, mix a capful of liquid dish detergent in a pail of water and pour it over one of your monitoring sites with a sprinkling can. Sod webworms and other pests will appear on the surface where they can be detected and counted.

The coffee can method is a great way to check for chinch bugs and involve your family in environmentally sound monitoring practices.

## THE COFFEE CAN METHOD

To detect chinch bugs, a common lawn pest, remove both ends from a large coffee can and push it a few inches into the sod. (If this is difficult, cut the sod first with a knife.) Fill the can with water. After about five minutes, all of the bugs will float to the surface. You can then count and identify them. The coffee can treatment is a perfect opportunity to involve your kids in environmentally sound and enjoyable monitoring.

## TROUBLESHOOTING
### When All Else Fails

It makes no sense to use any potion as a control, synthetic chemical or "organic." The reason for this is that prevention is the only true organic control. All potions—even Bt, rotenone and insecticidal soaps—have side effects that do harm to non-target species.

And, as mentioned earlier, "potion-based" controls only treat the *symptom*, they do not solve the problem.

If your lawn can't survive when the best, most climat-cally suitable varieties are selected and excellent maintenance procedures are followed, it's time to take up your turf and look for alternative ground covers.

If you have been following the maintenance program out-lined in this chapter and you have selected high-end grass blends that like your soil and climate, you shouldn't have problems with weeds, disease or insects. In fact, you may be astonished at the vigour of your lawn.

As a further preventive measure, you can also encourage pest-eating birds (see Chapter 2 for details) and attract ben-eficial bugs such as ladybugs and the praying mantis.

However, if you discover clear signs of trouble—yellow or brown patches, etc.—when you are out monitoring your lawn, the following information will tell you what those pests indicate about your main-tenance practices and how to correct them. If pests persist after corrective measures are taken, look for a more suit-able ground cover for that spot.

### Soap Drenches

Household soap drenches can be made by adding liquid dishwashing detergents to water. The drenches can be used to flush bugs out of their habitats for identifi-cation, if needed. Remember that soap kills the "good guys" too. Caution: Do not leave open containers of soap mixtures within the reach of children or pets.

### Ants

Ants are attracted to nutritionally poor, dry soils, with poor organic matter. While they are natural aerators, they can cause some damage under their hills. The dam-age is not severe, however, and they are regarded more as a household nuisance. Generally, if you increase the organic matter in your soil by top-dressing with compost after aeration, your soil will retain more moisture and the ant problem will take care of itself.

### Chinch bugs

These tiny red nymphs turn grey and develop wings as they mature. If you find more than 100-150 per square metre (10-15 per square foot) in any of your coffee can samples, you are probably slacking off in your lawn maintenance duties.

Chinch bugs like lots of thatch, 2 cm (¾ in.) or more, accompanied by dry roots and soil that is low or too rich in nitrogen.

To reduce chinch bugs in your lawns, aerate in spring and summer and dehatch in fall. Make sure you water deeply and infrequently and only in the mornings. Test your soil and correct for nitrogen deficiencies with slow-release, organic nitrogen sources, or better yet, let your clippings feed your lawn. Chances are, you have been over-feeding.

To keep them away next year, improve your feeding practices, replant with resistant varieties, or replace your turf with an alternative ground cover. Clover is a great substitute for turfgrass: the white-flowered Danish variety is smooth-spreading, low-growing, hardy, soft and likes all kinds of soil (including soil with low humus). And chinch bugs don't like it.

**Sod webworm moths**
If you notice a small white or dingy brown moth darting about the yard, this is probably the adult sod webworm, which hatches from a caterpillar in heavy thatch. The caterpillar skeletonizes and then cuts off grass blades. To check for sod webworms, use a soap drench of a capful of liquid detergent in a pail of water and sprinkle a 60-cm square (2-ft. square) area. The webworm caterpillars should crawl to the surface in five to 10 minutes. Rake them up and drop them in a bucket of insecticidal soap.

A healthy lawn is relatively safe from sod webworms if the larvae are present in small numbers, say, 20 or 30 in a square metre (two or three per square foot) But if your lawn is compacted, thatchy and dry, even one of these insects can cause problems. Aerate, top-dress with compost and endophytic grass seed and dethatch in the fall. Re-seeding will repel webworms and fill in damaged bare spots, crowding out the weeds.

Most caterpillars like lawns that are hot and dry during the day. Irrigate and top-dress with 6 mm (¼ in.) of weed-free compost. This should solve the problem completely.

## White grubs

In Canada and the USA, white grubs in your soil un
turf are usually the larvae of June or Japanese beet
more rarely, the European chafer. Damage usually a
in spring and fall as dead patches that lift easily.

The grubs are soft and white, with sectioned, C-shaped
bodies and reddish brown heads. They range in size from
6-75 mm (¼-3 in.) long. They are root feeders that prefer
compacted soil, chemical fertilizers and dry soil with a moist
thatch layer and weak grass roots. If they
are present in quantities greater than 50-
100 per square metre (5-10 per square
foot) they can cause patches of your lawn
to turn brown and die.

Once again, the best defence against all
three is a dense, healthy lawn. Dethatch,
aerate, add compost three times a year and
organic fertilizer once a year only, in the
fall. Water deeply and infrequently.
Japanese beetles in particular like moist
thatch to lay their eggs, but the eggs often
fail to hatch if surface soils are allowed to
dry between irrigations. When weeding,
take out the entire root, as grubs actually
prefer weed roots to grass roots.

### Sleuthing for Grubs:

You'll be able to determine if white grubs are the cause of any dead patches of lawn by cutting three sides of a 30-cm (1-ft.) square in your lawn at the edge of the damaged area. Gently lift the cut corner of your sod and peek at the roots. Collect any white grubs you see feeding on the roots or in the soil and take them to the appropriate authorities for identification. Replace sod and gently pat down.

## European crane fly or leatherjacket

This insect is actually harmless to lawns
unless its larvae are present in huge quantities: more than 250 per square metre (25
per square foot). It is extremely rare for the larvae to damage lawns as their natural predators are very successful.

So why the bad rap? The crane fly is one of those unfortunately fantastic looking species that evokes fear and
wonder—with the emphasis on fear.

People (mostly mothers, according to a very unscientific survey I've conducted on my travels) can't stand the sight of the adult flies, which look like mosquitoes on steroids, and are sure they will do creepy damage to their children or themselves.

Best defence? A healthy lawn. The larvae like thatch, fungi and compacted soil. Dethatch and aerate, make sure you water only in the mornings to allow the turf to dry before nightfall. Best reaction? Go to your library or the Internet and learn about these amazing beauties. Pick up a field guide on insects of North America (see **Further Reading**) and fall in love!

The next time you see a few fly up from your lawn, instead of running, shrieking, into the house and slamming the door in horror, take the kids by the hand and go over and look at the creatures. They don't bite and are actually gorgeous.

## Billbugs

This is primarily a warm-season insect that likes Bermuda and zoysia grasses and bluegrasses in the transitional zone. The adult is a brown or black weevil 6-13 mm (¼-½ in.) long, with a long snout. It feeds on grass stems.

Billbugs are attracted to compacted soil, shallow roots caused by too frequent, too shallow watering, thatch and organically poor soil. Sensing maintenance abuse here?

Dethatch in fall, aerate and add compost and water infrequently and very deeply to get those grass roots growing deep. Overseed with resistant varieties of perennial rye (see page 48 for best rye varieties).

## Aphids

Aphids, or green bugs, like stressed cool-season grasses. Stressed, because we are trying to grow them in shade and feeding them too much nitrogen. They like Kentucky bluegrass best, so make sure you get resistant varieties. These tiny bugs suck the juices out of grass blades. So ... stop feeding your lawn with chemical fertilizers and stop trying to grow Kentucky bluegrass—a sun lover—in the shade.

# Diseases

All lawn diseases can be directly attributed to a deficiency in your lawn's ecosystem, so the best prevention is proper lawn care. Monitor weekly to diagnose and treat a problem in its early stages, and NEVER mow a wet lawn.

Most diseases afflict lawns containing a large proportion of one species of fine turfgrasses, so remember to "blend" by top-dressing with a few of the recommended disease-resistant rye or tall fescues after aeration.

## Lawn Diseases

Most lawn diseases can be attributed to overly moist, shaded areas that have been mowed too short and too frequently. Increase drainage in your soil by aerating and top-dressing with compost and overseeding with shade resistant varieties. Water the grass less often, for longer periods so that the water soaks in to a depth of 20 cm (8 in.), and only in the early mornings.

If your lawn is in the shade, don't cut back the shade trees to give more sun to your lawn. In this era of increasing drought, ozone depletion and global warming, we are going to need all the shade we can get.

Rather than reducing the shade on your property, remove your turfgrasses and introduce moisture-loving native species, such as the many mosses that thrive in cool, damp, shady areas. Mosses are soft, green and need no maintenance. What could be better?

### Brown patch

Brown patch is a fungus that likes heavy thatch, humid shaded areas and high nitrogen levels in grass leaves. It appears as a circular or crescent-shaped, brown...well, patch. Dethatch, aerate, cut down on nitrogen and either prune back shade trees and shrubs (a crime, in my view) or stop trying to grow turfgrasses in those conditions (a far better solution). If you decide to keep on trying to grow grasses, overseed with resistant, endophytic perennial rye-grasses.

### Dollar spot

This common lawn fungus thrives on lawns with too little nitrogen and too much moisture above the soil—both products of improper watering and thatch build up. Dollar spot appears as small, circular, bleached dead spots of grass in spring or fall.

Aerate, top-dress with compost to improve soil health and drainage, dethatch in fall, test for nitrogen levels and amend accordingly with a slow-releasing organic product. Water in the early mornings and level out uneven spots in your lawn to prevent puddles. Dollar spot also loves grass cut too frequently and too short (see **Mowing**, page 60).

### Summer patch or "frog's eye"

This common fungus is attracted to a combination of humid weather and excess nitrogen. It appears as a patch of brown with tufts of green grass in the middle. Reduce nitrogen applications (put away that chemical fertilizer for good!) and overseed with endophytic ryegrasses.

### Mildew

Powdery mildew appears as a grey cobweb or white powdery growth, mainly on the upper surface of the grass blades. This fungus is most severe in shaded, wet areas with poor circulation.

Aerate, add compost, overseed with shade-tolerant grass seed and water only in the early mornings. Allow the soil to dry out completely between watering. Mow high, sharp and dry. If mildew persists, consider a more shade-tolerant ground cover for the area.

### Mushrooms and toadstools

These often appear in lawns during rainy spells in the summer. They are the aboveground growth of fungus that is growing on underground organic matter such as a buried stump or tree root. They are often the result of poor drainage or heavy shade.

They're harmless and they can be removed by raking. No other method of control will kill them without damaging your soil and putting your health at risk.

Mushrooms tend to like slightly acidic and calcium-deficient soils. Test the pH balance and calcium content in your soil. If necessary, add dolomite lime and wood ashes to bring the pH up to 6.5.

### Rust

Rust looks like it sounds; it likes warm, wet, infrequently mowed lawns. Poorly fertilized Kentucky bluegrass is its favourite dessert.

Aerate, add compost and a good organic nitrogen source (after testing your soil, of course) and overseed with shade- and rust-resistant perennial ryes and tall fescues.

Water less frequently, more deeply and only in the early mornings. Mow a bit more often; when the grass reaches 7.5 cm (3 in.), cut to 5 cm (2 in.) with newly sharpened blades. If rust persists, look for an alternative ground cover for that shady spot.

### Fusarium patch or pink snow mould

Another fungus that looks like its name: pink! This mould is attracted to compacted soil with too much moisture on the surface and poor drainage. It also loves grass that has been given a shot of chemical nitrogen late in the fall, its favourite feeding time.

Aerate your lawn, top-dress with compost and resistant grass seeds and feed with an organic fertilizer in early fall. Dethatch if necessary and remove the grass clippings from the last fall cut.

### Red thread

This fungus appears as red streaks on your grass blades. It loves grasses that are too high or too low in nitrogen, so the first thing to do is test your soil and feed organically, accordingly. Red thread also likes cool wet weather; not much you can do about that if you live in the Pacific Northwest but you can increase your soil drainage by aerating, adding compost and watering less frequently and more deeply. Remove thatch if it measures more than 6 mm (¼ in.) deep and overseed with resistant grass varieties. Another big hint: Don't mow wet grass. You will just spread whatever disease your grass has to every blade in your lawn.

And if red thread persists, plant a native ground cover that likes the wet conditions.

### Necrotic ring spot

Another disease that likes grasses that are mowed too short, too often. This one appears on your lawn looking suspiciously like summer patch or frog's eye—they are very hard to tell apart. Necrotic spot strikes healthy lawns, so it's usually a shock when it appears. Give your lawn a chance to grow longer between mowings. Remove any thatch and aerate and overseed with perennial ryes and tall fescues.

## Weeds

I hate to nag, but most weed problems can be attributed to soil compaction, excessive thatch, improper mowing practices and unbalanced pH and nutrient levels in your soil—in short, *people taking poor care of their lawns.*

If you keep your lawn healthy by practising the maintenance program outlined in this chapter, you'll have very few problems with weeds.

Weeds are opportunists: they move in when your preferred crop thins out, usually from a combination of poor species selection and poor maintenance. Check the following listings to learn what the weeds you find in your lawn are telling you about your soil, climate and gardening habits.

And remember, a "weed" is only a plant growing where you think it shouldn't. Maybe it's time to take a look at what you consider "good" and "bad." Some folks are actually encouraging dandelions, buttercups, clover, etc. to grow in their lawn, appreciating the colour and meadow-like appearance. Several North American cities now have official "dandelion festivals" where salad and wine recipes are exchanged and lawn alternatives displayed.

Some gardeners are intentionally introducing native grasses and ground covers to naturalize their yards, inviting native birds and butterflies back into the community by doing so. Think outside the green carpet!

## Crabgrass
The bane of suburbia in the 50s, this low-growing annual has shallow roots, making it a good candidate for hand-pulling as a control. When crabgrass appears, it means that your soil is nutrient deficient and compacted. It also means that you have been mowing too short, stressing the grass plants to the point of death. As they have thinned out, the crabgrass has moved in.

So: hand-pull, aerate three times a year, add compost and organic nutrients according to your soil test results and put those mower blades *up*. Sharpen them too, while you're at it.

## Common plantain (and pretty well all broad-leaved weeds)
Plantain is a broad-leaved weed that was once called missionary plant, because it followed priests wherever they went in the New World to bring religion to the First Nations. This plant, like all broad-leaved weeds (hawkweed, etc.) moves in when your soil is compacted, poorly nourished and too wet, causing your grass to thin out.

Control is simple: Aerate, add compost to improve oxygen content and drainage, test your soil and feed organically according to the results and water less frequently, more deeply.

**Clover: pro or con?**
Clovers are actually extremely useful for lawns. They attract beneficial nectar-feeding insects and fix nitrogen in your soil. In fact, clover is often added to grass-seed mixes intentionally and in some cases planted instead of lawns. This is because clover is drought- and pest-resistant, strong and hearty, low growing and green. If the proper species is selected, it provides a great yard cover. Pest or guest?

## Clover

Clover can grow in alkaline or acidic soil and loves dry, nutrient deficient lawns with thinning grasses. You can prevent clover from taking over your lawn by adjusting pH, aerating and adding compost to improve drainage and feeding your soil with organic nutrients according to test results.

But wait. All clover is extremely beneficial to lawns. It fixes nitrogen in the soil and is often planted as a green manure—a winter crop that is turned under in spring to fertilize the soil. Clover attracts beneficial nectar-feeding insects and adds texture and colour to your lawn. In fact, clover is often added to lawn seed mixes purposely.

The plants are hearty, low growing, resistant to insects and diseases, provide soft playing areas and are beautiful. Think twice before you decide to do away with this "weed."

**Dandelion Patrol:**
Some of the more zealous homeowners we talked to spoke of taking off dandelion heads that had gone to seed—by hand. The advice was to use a plastic bag to cover the head of the offender and pinch it off while still "in the bag." If you miss mowing the lawn before the weeds form seed heads, this may be worth a try. Get your kids involved—you can even base their allowance on the number of seed heads/dandelion roots they present to you.
Caution: Avoid inhaling seeds, as they can be an allergen.

## Creeping Charlie or moneywort

Creeping Charlie likes shade, moisture, compacted soil and thatch—all the stuff that turfgrasses hate. So you can aerate, add compost, water deeply and less frequently and grow shade-tolerant grasses, or, encourage Charlie to stay.

This "weed" is a member of the primrose family that spreads by trailing stems. Small coloured flowers bloom profusely in midsummer above dark green leaves. One variety has golden leaves and makes a stunning ground cover in its own right. Why try to convince a lawn to grow in dark moist areas when you can have the beautiful creeping Charlie?

## Dandelions

Along with crabgrass, dandelions got their bad rap in the 50s as the sign of a yard cared for by a slacker, a lazy, bad person who was not house-proud. Rubbish!

Dandelions are beautiful, beneficial herbs, high in vitamins E and C, iron and potassium. Dandelions also attract a natural microscopic predator, the parasitic wasp, that helps to keep down caterpillar, fly maggot and earwig populations.

Dandelions are attracted to soil that is low in pH and nutritionally "challenged." They also prefer soil on the sandy side and thinning turf grass.

If you can't learn to love your dandelions (they are great in salads, nutritious and make fabulous wine), hand-pick to the root, balance your soil pH, aerate and top-dress with compost and endophytic ryegrasses. Make sure you cut your grass before dandelions go to seed.

**Pocketful of Rye**

Whenever you weed, keep a pocket full of perennial ryes and some good tall fescue seeds. As the weed is pulled, sprinkle some of the grass seed on the spot and water. The rye, especially, will germinate and sprout quickly, filling in the space before another weed can move in.

### Thistle

This plant is difficult to eradicate. Thistle has a deep root that cannot be destroyed easily: it must be dug out completely. Any little pieces left in the ground will produce new plants. It's best to hand pull these plants when they are young and small. Fill in the hole left behind with some compost and seed immediately with a fast-growing ryegrass to cover the area.

## A FINAL WORD

It is not necessary—or environmentally desirable—to continue drenching your lawn in toxic chemicals. You and your family can enjoy a healthy, beautiful yard that is organically maintained by following the steps outlined above. Learn to love the beautiful and diverse insect and bird life that will flourish once you stop using toxins. And if buttercups or primrose appear, don't panic. Make them the centrepiece for your next picnic.

# 5

# PESTICIDE-FREE VEGETABLES

*T*he only ways to be sure that you are not eating pesticides along with your fruit and vegetables are to buy certified organic produce, or to grow your own. A few of your efforts may go to bugs, but the sacrifice will be worth it. Plant a few extra and almost all of your crop will survive unmolested to feed you, your family and friends deliciously and safely.

And of course, select fruits and vegetables that will do well in your soil and climate.

## YOUR GARDEN PLOT
A place in the sun

Vegetable and fruit gardens need plenty of sunlight, good soil and good drainage. Pick a spot with southern exposure, away from shade trees and buildings.

In general, soil preparation is as outlined in Chapter 3. But take note: plants differ in their pH and nutrient requirements. Before you add organic fertilizers, lime or flowers of sulphur, investigate the specific requirements of the plants you intend to grow. Tomatoes need acidic soil, for example, while cabbage likes alkaline soil. And, of course, *test your* soil to find out what's in it and what it needs to feed those hungry veggies and fruit plants.

As you prepare your soil, laying on organic fertilizers and compost, leave the soil in raised beds or mounds. Raised beds make plants easier to feed, weed and water. They also insure good drainage and help to keep roots cooler in hot weather and warmer in cool climates. If you make your beds small enough to reach the middle comfortably from each side, you eliminate soil compaction due to human traffic between rows. This minimizes the need for aeration.

Plant to ensure sun lovers get enough light, and shade lovers are protected by taller plants.

## COMPANION PLANTING
With friends like these, you'll have fewer enemies

Companion planting is a basic principle of organic gardening. Many plants repel bugs and provide natural protection if they're planted beside susceptible species. Some plants help to feed their neighbours by making trace elements more easily available to the roots.

For example, the roots of French marigolds repel nematodes that infest many garden plants, including tomatoes and potatoes. Plant marigolds throughout the garden and in consolidated blocks in beds that will grow tomatoes next year.

Inter-planting potatoes and collards reduces potato beetle damage. Garlic plants repel the larvae of many harmful insects and can be planted next to anything except onions. Onion plants repel many insects and can be scattered throughout the garden.

On the other hand, some plants are actually bad for each other when planted too close together. Related plants like cauliflower and broccoli should be separated to discourage bugs that like the same family. (Check out Louise Riotte's *Carrots Love Tomatoes* in **Further Reading**.)

Then there is the whole concept of "trap" planting. This entails planting to *attract* pests *to* a specific plant as a sacrificial or trap plant, so that the pests will leave another plant alone. An example of this is planting nasturtiums in a block a few feet away from lettuce. Aphids prefer nasturtiums and will be kept busy eating their favourite dish, while your lettuce grows to maturity. You just have to find out what the pest that's eating your crop likes even better and put some of that nearby.

And some gardeners inter-plant all their crops in a great garden mixture to confuse predators as well. The hodgepodge effect: one broccoli plant beside one lettuce, beside one garlic, next to another broccoli, next to a few carrots and a tomato. The diversity of this system works well to deter pests, but is a bit tricky, as different plants have different soil and feeding requirements. If you want to plant a mixed garden, make sure companions are grouped together and plants that like the same pH and nutrients are grouped together.

## PLANTING YOUR GARDEN

As you sow...

If you are planting in anything except the hodge-podge design, you need to map your plantings to make sure you know where to rotate your crops to next season. Make a map of where each crop will go in your garden, making sure to build in the companion, soil requirement and exposure principles outlined above.

If you change your mind as you plant, be sure to mark the changes on the map, too. Keep the map in a safe place for reference until next year's garden is planted. Now you are ready to sow.

Choose disease-resistance plant varieties and *crops that are suited to your climate.* Try to find organic heritage seeds, to insure the continuation of the species on the planet and to thwart the attempts of huge multinational corporations—the same ones that make synthetic pesticides—to patent all life forms for profit. (Don't get me started.)

Plant as recommended on the seed packet, indoors in potting soil, or outdoors once the soil is warm. If you're starting seed indoors, be sure to "harden off" the seedlings to prepare them gently for the temperature changes of the great outdoors. Start by putting the pots outside in the warm sun during the day and bringing them in each night for a few days. Then, once the nights are warm enough, leave the plants outdoors overnight for a few days before actually planting them in your prepared bed.

**Seeds and Plants, the Proper Choice:** Proper plant selection is *the* first step you take to insure healthy crops. If you try to grow eggplant in a cool-summer climate, all the chemicals on the world are not going to save the situation. Select disease-resistant varieties and *plant seeds and crops that are appropriate to your soil and climate, just the way it is.* I can't say this enough.

Follow your garden plan, planting companions next to each other and separating related species to discourage bugs that are attracted to the family. Plant flowers throughout the vegetable garden to attract beneficial insects and birds that will feed on undesired garden raiders.

Erect supports for beans, tomatoes, peas, etc., before you plant, so the roots of your plants will not be damaged later.

If you are sowing seeds directly into the beds, place them close together and thin out the seedlings as they require more space. Water gently with a sprinkling can and mulch until seeds have sprouted (see **Mulching**, page 80). Keep the planted area moist until seeds germinate and you see the tiny plants push through.

Once the plants have pushed through the soil, move the mulch back from the stems to prevent rot, but still keep roots moist.

For transplantation of seedlings, sow them as close to one another as possible to shade out weeds and then thin as they require more room. Dig the hole in the bed, water it and then remove the seedling from its pot. Gently water the roots as you place the seedling in the hole, cover with soil and tamp down gently. Water the area gently each day for a week, until the roots have established themselves in the new soil, then deeply and infrequently.

Always transplant early in the day or under cloud cover to protect the roots while they are exposed. Mulch around the seedlings, making sure the mulch does not touch the stems.

You can plant gorgeous flowers, shrubs, trees and vines around your home and veggie garden to invite "pest control on the wing" right to your doorstep. For a list of plants and the birds they will bring, see pages 24-26.

## THE SEVEN-STEP MAINTENANCE PROGRAM
How does your veggie garden grow?

## 1. Mulching, the protective blanket

Mulches are coverings laid directly on garden beds to keep weeds down, retain moisture and warmth in the soil and hasten germination of seeds. Unless you live in a very wet and cool climate, mulches are generally a fantastic aid to the organic gardener. They cut maintenance time down to a fraction.

Mulches can be made from organic matter such as straw, grass clippings, seaweed, compost, bark chips or sawdust. Avoid hay or unsterilized manures, which harbour weed seeds, and anything which may have been treated with pesticides.

Organic mulches can be applied in thin layers over planted seeds to hasten sprouting of plants, placed around transplanted seedlings to cover beds and spread on your beds after the fall harvest to reduce leaching of nutrients over the winter.

Organic mulches add nutrients slowly to the soil as they break down. The disadvantages are that they may attract slugs, earwigs and some fungi and moulds in cool, wet climates. In areas of the country with short or cool growing seasons, organic mulches can insulate the soil, keeping it too cool and rotting the plant roots. In these conditions, it is better to water uncovered beds using soaker hoses as needed instead of mulching, or to use landscape fabric.

Sawdust and wood chips are good idea along garden paths to keep weeds down.

Mulches can also be made from inorganic substances such as black plastic, gravel, or landscaping fabric.

## 2. Watering: Soak the soil, not the foliage

Most gardens need a thorough soaking at least once every 10 days. The water should soak the soil to a depth of 2.5 cm (1 in.) below the roots. There are many commercially available probes that will let you know how deep the water is going, but if you place a cup in the soil sunk to the rim and allow water from your drip system to flow into it, you'll know you have watered sufficiently, even for the most deeply rooted veggies, when the cup is 5 cm (2 in.) full.

Make sure to water the soil, not the foliage. Perforated soaker hoses are the best bet: You get more moisture where it is needed—in the soil—and foliage is not moistened. Adjust the water pressure so you get a dribble rather than a spray.

**Did I Mention ...**
I can't say this enough: *Water the soil*, not the plants. If the leaves and fruits of your plants become wet, they will burn as the sun evaporates the moisture and will be very susceptible to moisture-loving insects and diseases including moulds and blights. Wet leaves and fruits cause a *huge* percentage of plant problems.

Water early in the morning to avoid evaporation and to allow soaking-in time before nightfall. This will also discourage slugs and other water-seeking beasties. If your plants show signs of leaf wilt, water the surrounding soil immediately, mulch and readjust your watering schedule to prevent the soil from drying out between applications.

## 3. Feeding: It is what it eats

Test your soil and then add amendments after the soil has warmed up in the spring, by laying on huge amounts of compost, well rotted manure and organic fertilizers. Don't stop there. Even if your soil is perfectly balanced for pH and nutrients at the beginning of the season, you need to keep adding compost as your garden grows. Compost can be added right over your organic mulches or landscaping fabric.

Use well-rotted manure and compost throughout the season as a side dressing (laid along the side of the plant, under the outermost foliage—the drip line) for members of the cabbage family and all leaf crops. The exceptions for this treatment are members of the legume family such as peas and beans.

## 4. Aeration: The breath of life

Believe it or not, your plants and soil need a steady supply of oxygen—just like we do—to stay healthy. Establish clear footpaths that are outside the range of root growth to avoid soil compaction. You can also aerate your beds—gently— once or twice a month, being careful not to damage the

roots. Use a spiked roller, available at most garde
stores, a trowel or a hoe and gently cultivate the so
your plants. Add compost around the base of t
directly below the drip-line and water.

Raised beds are best for avoiding compaction.

## 5. Putting your garden to bed

After you harvest your crops, make sure you clean your garden beds well for the winter ahead. This means removing
all dead leaves, roots from this year's crops, etc. to discourage
pests that hibernate, feed or lay eggs on garden debris in
the "down" season. Don't leave dead plants in your soil over
the winter.

After you harvest and clean, lay on a good amount of
compost, seaweed and rotted manure and top with straw.
Your beds will be cozy and feed slowly over the winter.

## 6. Green manures: Winter food, spring fodder

Another great option to pamper and build up your soil over
the winter months is to plant a "green manure." Lay on the
compost and well rotted manure, then plant a fast growing
nitrogen-fixing crop such as clover or ryegrass. This will
provide your soil with nitrogen through the winter and with
organic matter when turned under in spring. It will protect
your topsoil from the erosion of winter snow, winds and
rain and increase absorptive and biochemical processes in
your soil. Your garden centre or seed supplier can assist you
in choice of a green manure crop.

Plant as soon as possible after the last harvest and at least
one or two weeks before the first killing frost.

NOTE: If grubs of June or Japanese beetles have been a
problem, avoid green manures for season or two until the larvae have been eradicated. Instead, turn your soil over. Those
grubs not eaten by birds will move to less disturbed areas.

## 7. Crop rotation: Musical beds

Keep your garden map from one season to the next so you can remember where everything was planted and rotate your crops accordingly. You want to plant family members in beds where no relatives lived last year and make sure that plants that were heavy feeders go to beds that were most recently occupied by light feeders. Crop rotation helps to keep down predators and to rest and replenish your soil.

Plant companions next to each other and separate related varieties such as cauliflower or broccoli to discourage bugs and diseases that are partial to any one family. Keep a map of this year's garden and take care not to rotate family members to each other's beds next season.

An example? Carrots are unrelated to lettuce and can be planted next season in this year's lettuce beds. Broccoli and cauliflower, however, are related and should not be rotated to each other's beds this season or next. Broccoli and cauliflower should also be planted a few rows away from each other in any one season. For further reading on crop rotation see *Rodale's Encyclopedia of Organic Gardening* (**Further Reading**).

## TIPS ON TRANSITION
Weaning the garden off chemicals

If you have been using chemical fertilizers and pesticides in your garden, your soil is deficient in organic matter and some important trace elements. The good bugs have been destroyed, together with the micro-organisms in your soil that help to repel disease and make nutrients available to plant roots.

To rebuild the soil and micro-organism colonies, add compost and well rotted manure in the spring about a month before planting. If this means planting a little late, plant a little late. Continue to add compost and well-rotted manure as a side dressing under the outermost foliage of your plants (the drip-line) throughout the season.

At the same time, follow all the advice outlined in this chapter, including soil testing and the addition of organic fertilizers as required. These amendments will help your soil and plants through withdrawal from the chemical diet.

## TROUBLESHOOTING
When pests persist

I may sound like a broken record on this one, but let me play it one more time:

- "Pests" are only pests because they are competing with us for what WE want.

- Everything in your yard is there because you put it there, or because it was attracted to something, be it poor soil, overly-nitrogenized plants, heavy shade, etc. *Pay attention* to what is attracted to your yard; it will teach you volumes about the ecosystem.

**Transition Tip:**
You may experience some problems during the transition, or "detox" period, but *please* resist the temptation to bring out the chemical arsenal to try and remedy the problem.

Understand that until your soil regains its health, the built-in beneficial organisms and needed trace minerals will take awhile to regain a foothold. Further chemical abuse will just slow or stop this rehabilitation and you will be destroying any progress you have made.

- To avoid problems with competitors (pests) in the first place, plant species that like your soil and climate just the way it is, then *take good care of them,* following the steps outlined, above.

- Look at your plants every week, so you can spot a problem before it gets out of hand. Then take remedial maintenance actions.

- The Rule of Potions: All potions—organic or synthetic—damage innocent bystanders, so if you have a serious problem that improved maintenance can not solve, replace the besieged plant with something more suited to your growing conditions.

## Weeds

If you follow the maintenance program and preventive measures described in this chapter, weeds should not be a serious problem.

If weeds appear, they are an indicator that your soil is nutritionally unbalanced, or that your maintenance has thinned out your plants to allow weeds in. This phenomenon is discussed in the previous chapter on lawns. If you have weeds, check out pages 72 to 75 find out what they are telling you about your soil and how to remedy the situation.

Remove weeds by hand and take corrective measures to prevent their return.

The easiest time for weeding is right after watering or rain—the roots come away easily. Remove weed debris immediately from the garden to prevent re-rooting.

Mulches, organic or inorganic, go a long way to prevent weeds from choking out your garden plants. If you need added moisture, use organic mulches. If your garden is already very moist, use landscape fabric, black plastic or gravel.

## Insects

If you select regionally appropriate plants, interplant and follow the maintenance steps outlined in this chapter, insects should not be a problem. Again, the presence of a particular predator will tell you what you need to do in terms of improving your maintenance. Some of the more common insects are listed below, along with information on what they are trying to tell you and what to do once you've got the message.

Landscape fabric is gaining popularity as a shield to insulate and keep bugs off garden beds. Many landscape fabrics that are used over rows as a protection can now be recycled. Make sure you have a recycling outlet for the fabric before you buy it.

Some insects, notably ladybugs and praying mantises, consume hundreds if not thousands of harmful predator bugs. If they are not already residents of your garden, plant their favourite plants to attract them. I used to recommend purchase of such bugs. However, this in itself has caused problems. Ladybugs have been uprooted from their own colonies, bred and flown across the country—not exactly environmentally friendly. Ladybugs not from this country have been introduced as pest control and are taking over native ladybugs' habitat. The best bet is to attract native pest predators by planting the regional flowers and plants that they live or feed on.

If you find an insect you don't recognize during your monitoring, look it up in a good reference book, take a sample to your local gardening centre or send a sample to a university or government lab. Do not use insecticides, synthetic or organic. You will be destroying non-target, beneficial insects that keep your soil and plants healthy. Even insecticidal soaps have non-target casualties, including ladybugs. And pyrethrin, the chrysanthemum-based pesticide, is also toxic to non-target species.

Instead, design the pest out by removing the conditions that have attracted it, or make or purchase mechanical traps

## Don't Buy Bugs

I no longer recommend purchase of "beneficial" insects and organisms as pest control, since this causes as many problems as it solves. One of Canada's provincial governments found this out the hard way. Thinking to solve an aphid problem organically, the government purchased, imported and released thousands of Asian ladybugs to do their worst–and they have. Turns out they bite humans, are reproducing at a great rate, swarming homes and taking out local ladybugs. Not good! The best bet is to attract native (local) beneficials by planting the regional flowers and plants that they live or feed on.

and barriers. If insects continue to be a problem, it's time to reconsider your choice of crop.

## Aphids (see also page 68)

Aphids are attracted to highly nitrogenized plants in soil that is poor in organic matter. Stop using high nitrogen chemical fertilizers and add compost to your soil as a side dressing.

Encourage the presence of aphids' natural enemies—ladybugs, praying mantises and warblers—by planting nasturtiums, etc. Plant garlic, chives, coriander and anise throughout the garden as repellents.

Make or purchase aphid traps. These are basically pieces of cardboard covered with a yellow sticky substance. Hang the traps about the garden, or place a yellow dish full of soapy water in the garden. Monitor your catch. If you're catching or drowning beneficial bugs along with the aphids, remove the traps and dishes.

## Asparagus beetle

Pretty to look at! Metallic blue, 6.3mm (¼ in.) long, with yellow-orange squares on each wing cover. Both adults and larvae eat foliage and tender asparagus shoots. They hibernate in garden debris, then emerge in spring to feed. They also like plants low in phosphorus. So: clean up your garden in the fall, removing overwintering grounds for this pest, and test and add bone meal/phosphate rock as required. You can also interplant with nasturtiums, calendula and tomatoes.

### Cabbage worms and cabbage loopers

These worms are 4 cm (1½ in.) long, pale green, with light stripes down their backs. Its distinctive way of moving—it loops or doubles up as it crawls—makes it easy to identify. Eggs are green and white and laid on leaf surfaces. If you see 'em, scrape 'em off.

Cabbage worms and loopers like slightly acidic soil. They attack members of the cabbage family, peas, lettuce and tomatoes. Fight back by making your soil more alkaline, except for tomatoes, which like the acid. Hand-pick the worms. Apply wood ashes in a ring at the base of infected plants. You can also plant mint, catnip, thyme and rosemary as deterrents.

### Carrot weevil

Copper-coloured, 3 mm (⅛ in.) long with a protruding snout, the larva is a small white grub with a white head. These weevils like carrots, parsnip, celery, parsley and...weeds.

The adults overwinter in weeds, so control is simple: keep your garden clean!

### Colorado potato beetle

These beetles are yellow with a broad, convex back. They adore potatoes, as their name suggests, but will also happily feed on eggplant, tomatoes, peppers and petunias.

Your best defence is to plant resistant varieties and when monitoring, check plants for clusters of yellow eggs on the underside of the leaves.

### Corn borers and earworms

Corn borers are striped, light yellow, green or brown with yellow heads. They worms can grow up to 5 cm (2 in.) and the adult moth has greyish-brown wings with dark lines. The worms feed on the buds and new leaves of plants, the silk tassels of corn and the fruit of tomatoes, beans, cabbage, broccoli and lettuce, especially if your soil is nutrient-deficient.

Test your soil and feed organically, accordingly. Buy

resistant plant varieties. As a further prevention, apply 20 drops of mineral oil to the inside tip of each ear of corn with a paintbrush or eyedropper after the silks have wilted. If that doesn't work, pick them off by hand.

Corn is a heavy feeder. Interplant your corn with legumes to keep the nutrient level balanced and the borers and earworms at bay. Rotate the crop in next year's garden.

### Cutworms

These plump, smooth-bodied, soil-dwelling worms love young transplants, especially those from the cabbage family, but they will not pass up beans and tomatoes. For prevention, keep your garden free of weeds and grass during fall months when cutworms are laying their eggs.

Plant sunflowers. They are beautiful and attract and trap cutworms. Tansy and marigolds repel cutworms. Better yet, do all of the above and place tar paper, cardboard, or tin can collars around transplants, sunk in the soil to 2.5 cm (1 in.) to prevent the worms from reaching plant stems. (See diagram.)

For added protection, place collars around your vegetable seedlings to prevent cutworm damage. It works! You can make them from tarpaper or cardboard milk cartons and rip them open to discard after the seedlings have matured. Bushy plants like lettuce won't tolerate collars, but most others will benefit.

### Earwigs

These brown, beetle-like insects with the famous forceps on their tails eat the larvae of many harmful insects and only occasionally attack vegetables. They love excess moisture, especially in dark places. So make sure you water in the early mornings, so that the top of the soil is not wet at night.

If they are still a problem, leave a hollow tube or a piece of bamboo containing a few drops of water at one end of your garden overnight. The earwigs will crawl inside and can be tapped into a bucket of soapy water in the morning.

### Flea beetles

Flea beetles are just like they sound: black, hard-cased beetles that jump like fleas. They love it hot and dry, especially in combination with low soil nutrients. They are partial to corn, eggplant, potatoes, spinach and tomatoes.

So test your soil and amend accordingly. Keep your beds mulched in drought conditions, interplant preferred varieties with garlic and other strong-smelling plants and flowers. Plant your crops thickly: beetles don't like shade.

If all else fails, use garlic spray, hand-pick the beetles and rotate your crops.

### White grubs (June beetle, Japanese beetle and European chafer larvae)

These prehistoric-looking, soft, white, sectional-bodied grubs with reddish brown heads can reach 7.5 cm (3 in.). They are root feeders and are attracted to soil that has most recently been a law... in fact, you probably have these predators if your garden was a lawn in the last season or so. Grubs can take three years to mature into beetles and all the while, they will be feeding on roots.

If you find them during your monitoring you will have to aerate your soil, big time. The more "disturbed" your soil, the faster they will move on, so aerate, aerate, aerate! If you have a major infestation, the harsh reality is that you should probably wait a year to plant crops of any kind and, in the meantime, turn the soil over, leave it a couple of weeks and turn over again. Robins will feast on the bounty!

Stop when the soil becomes too cold to work, or when most of the grubs appear to have gone, whichever comes

### An "okay" potion: garlic spray

Because it repels by odour rather than killing, garlic spray is one of the few potions I still recommend. But be careful not to make it too strong: no more than two cloves to a litre or quart of water, or you'll burn your plant leaves.

Put two cloves of peeled and chopped garlic in your blender with a litre/quart of water and zap for 30 seconds. Place the liquid in a spray bottle and apply to affected plants.

This will repel many predators.

first. Start rebuilding micro-organism communities by adding lots of well-rotted compost and manure. Don't put in a green manure; let the soil rest for the remainder of the season and plant next spring.

If you find the grubs in the soil around your corn, immediately plant geraniums and next year, plant legumes in the same spot.

## Rebecca's Corner

My friend Rebecca spends hours in her Pacific Northwest vegetable garden each day, observing and learning from the ground up, so to speak. She has come up with a couple of brilliant "cultural practices" that really work for slugs.

She makes a jumbled ring of cut pieces of thick, Himalayan blackberry branches around her raised beds about 15 cm (6 in.) high. This crown of thorns is just too daunting for the gastropods.

Two summers ago, a bale of ruined hay that had been untied never made it onto the beds, but sat beside the garden in a sunny spot. Garden snakes began to use the loosened bale as their favourite shedding medium and stayed in her beds to eat slugs. Now that the word has been passed around the 'nabe, snakes come from far and wide to shed their skins (a bonus: whole snake-skins), bask in the sun and eat slugs. Perfect!

### Slugs and snails

These slimy gastropods will eat almost anything in a wet garden, but they are very easy to control. Slugs and snails love moisture and darkness, so make sure that your watering is done in the early morning so that your soil has a chance to dry out by nightfall. Pick the slugs and snails off by hand each morning.

Make plant collars of window screen with jagged tops to keep the slugs from climbing over.

*Do not use slug bait.* It is *extremely* toxic—and attractive—to pets and wildlife. Moreover, slugs will become immune to it and breed bait-resistant sluglets.

## Spider mites

Members of the spider family, spider mites appear as tiny red dots on the underside of leaves. They like all kinds of vegetables, but are usually kept low enough in numbers by their natural predators to prevent serious damage to your crops.

## Squash bugs

These brown or black "stink bugs" (named for a reason, okay?) love cucumbers, squash and pumpkins. Their brick-red egg clusters are laid on leaves. They like garden debris and will live in weeds while feeding on your crops. So get with the maintenance program! Remove crop and weed debris from the garden. And make sure to plant your squash in a different place next season.

Companion-plant these vegetables with nasturtiums, radishes and marigolds. Place boards or shingles near the infested plants to trap the bugs overnight.

## Thrips

These tiny, dark, threadlike insects like flowers, beans and most weeds. Keep weed levels down, remove crop thinnings and weed debris from the garden as soon as they are harvested.

A mulch of aluminum foil repels thrips. Place a flat circle of aluminum foil around the plant with a slit cut for the stems.

## Tomato hornworms

These lime-green worms like tomatoes, dill, eggplant, peppers and potatoes. They reach 1 cm (½ in.) in length and are easily controlled by hand picking. Plant marigolds, borage and nicandra as natural deterrents.

Brachanoid wasps attach themselves in white oval cocoons to the ends of hornworms. If you see a cocoon on a worm, do not destroy it. The hatching wasps will do more than their share of pest control.

## Diseases

Diseases in vegetable gardens are relatively rare. They most often attack tomatoes, potatoes and members of the cabbage family such as broccoli and cauliflower. Buy resistant varieties and remember that the best-fed and best-tended plants suffer least, so keep your soil and plants healthy.

Most diseases appear in mid to late season, when the weather is hot, foliage is dense and disease-spreading insects (notably aphids) are moving from plant to plant.

Placing blight-susceptible plants, such as tomatoes, too close together reduces air circulation and will bring on blight, especially in warm, humid conditions.

Your best defence is excellent plant care:

- In humid weather, remove organic mulch a short distance from plant stems until the weather gets drier.

- Make sure that there is enough air circulating around your tomato plants and any others that are susceptible to airborne blight.

- *Water the soil, not the foliage.*

- If disease strikes a plant, be ruthless: Remove it immediately from the garden to the barbecue. Then wash your hands with soap and water and clean any garden tools with rubbing alcohol.

## Bacterial Diseases

Bacterial diseases appear in hot, humid weather and attack non-resistant varieties. Choose resistant plants. Make sure the leaves and stems of your plants are dry—*don't water the plant, water the soil.* Make sure there is plenty of air circulating around each plant ... don't crowd them in.

If disease does appear, destroy all affected plants, rotate your crops and buy fresh seed next year.

**Blight** causes pea and tomato stems and leaves to turn purple or black. Small water soaked spots appear on leaves and pea pods.

**Bacterial ring** affects potatoes, turning leaf edges inward. A dark ring appears on the tubers just inside the skin.

**Soft rot** affects lettuce, cabbage and carrots, turning them soft and pulpy.

## Fungal Diseases

Fungal diseases include club root (cabbage family), black leg (cabbage and tomatoes) and downy mildew (onions, lettuce and peas). Like bacterial diseases, they appear in hot, humid weather.

Again, select resistant varieties, ensure good air circulation around each plant by thinning, remove mulches in humid weather and destroy all affected plants. Aerate your beds and rotate all crops for next year's garden.

**Keep It Clean**
Don't spread disease: Make sure to wash your hands thoroughly after handling diseased plants, especially before you tend to their uninfected neighbors. Dip any garden tools that come into contact with diseased foliage in rubbing alcohol.

# A FINAL WORD

There's nothing so delicious as vegetables eaten moments after they are picked from your garden. And there's nothing so reassuring as knowing they you have raised them organically. Many gardeners in Canada and the United States who have practised organic gardening for decades have found that if they follow practical plant selection and maintenance rules, a few plants might be sacrificed to pests, but more than enough vegetables reach their tables—harvested from rich, healthy and safe soil.

# 6

## ORGANIC ORNAMENTALS

*O*rnamental flowers, ground covers, shrubs, vines and trees can grace your grounds in good health without the use of toxic chemicals. As with lawns and vegetables, the key to healthy, pest-resistant ornamentals is healthy soil. Review Chapter 2 before following the advice in this chapter.

Make sure you choose varieties of ornamentals that are suited to your climate, soil and light conditions, your particular yard and the particular spot you have in mind to place them in. Trying to make a sun-lover thrive in the shade or a moisture-loving plant do well in a desert just won't work. Regionally propagated, disease-resistant seeds, bulbs and plants—especially the many thousands of gorgeous, colourful plants that are native to your region—make a lot more sense and will give you years of beauty without environmentally disruptive, wasteful, or toxic remedies.

Choose individual plants carefully, too. Before you buy, examine each plant for wilt, blackened leaves, egg clusters under the leaves, insects flying up out of the soil in the pot and other signs of disease and pest damage. Don't accept a specimen with broken branches, scraped bark, or a ruptured root ball. You will be asking for maintenance chores in the very near future.

For advice on roses, check the special section in this chapter.

## SOIL PREFERENCE
Coffee, tea or bone meal?

Most evergreens (cedars, rhododendrons, azaleas, yews, junipers) like slightly acidic soil that is not too high in nitrogen.

Deciduous trees and shrubs (those that lose their leaves in winter) generally like soils that are richer in nitrogen (organic, of course) and organic matter supplied by compost. Proper drainage is essential. Some, such as apple, cherry and oak, prefer slightly acidic soils, while others, such as crabapple, do best in alkaline conditions. Check with your nursery.

A soil test is necessary to determine the pH and nutritional balance of your soil before you add lime or specific nutrient amendments. (See **Resources**.) Some plants are heavy feeders and will like applications of compost spread around the drip-line a few times throughout the season.

## PLANTING
Right time, right place

Plant ornamentals in early spring before new growth appears, or in fall, during their dormant period. Spring planting gives plants with delicate root systems the chance to establish themselves during the warm summer months. Be sure to select a spot carefully, in adequate sun and in an area with good drainage.

The importance of protecting the roots before planting can't be overemphasized. Buy plants only when you are ready to plant to avoid exposing roots to the air. If this is not possible, leave the plants in the pots for up to two weeks. Any longer may crowd the roots too much.

You can unwrap and then cover the roots of shrubs and trees with mud and stand them in the shade until you are ready to plant. Mudding also protects the roots if you are planting on a hot, windy day. Or you can dig a temporary trench and bury the roots until you are ready to plant.

When planting, dig a hole deep and wide enough so the roots will not be cramped. The hole needs to be only slightly deeper and wider than the plant's root spread.

Recent research has proven that, for most varieties of shrubs and trees, it is not a good idea to add fertilizers, peat moss, or other soil boosters to the soil filling your hole. Roses and fruit trees are the exceptions.

With your plants in place, fill half the hole with soil and water. When the water has seeped in, add the remaining earth and tamp it down firmly. Apply a mulch around the stem or trunk, but not touching it. Water again. Create a shallow well with earth around the trunk of trees after planting to assist with irrigation.

Trees should be staked only if they are planted in extremely windy spots. Otherwise, you'll actually be weakening your tree trunk.

Young trees with thin bark (maples, beeches, birches, etc.) will benefit if the trunks are wrapped in burlap for protection against sunscald, windburn and certain types of tree borers. Use 15-cm (6-in.) strips of burlap with brown waxed freezer paper on the inside. Starting at the bottom, wrap up the trunk into the branches (see illustration, page 96). The wrapping may be left on for one year and then removed. If you do not remove the wrapping at this time, your bark will begin to decay.

## MAINTENANCE
Three keys to beautiful ornamentals

## 1. Pruning
Trees and shrubs need pruning for various reasons;

- to correct or repair damage
- to encourage fruit and flower production
- to direct or control growth
- to help a transplanted tree or shrub
  adjust to its new surroundings.

The season for pruning varies with the type of plant and results you wish to achieve.

Many homeowners pull out the chemical arsenal if their trees and shrubs are doing poorly when a good haircut will solve the problem. Removing dead or diseased branches is the best remedy.

Following are a few general pointers on pruning shrubs, hedges and fruit trees. For further reading see **Resources** at the back of the book.

### Tools
Always use the proper tool for your pruning job and make sure that the cuts are clean, not jagged. For branches thinner than 1 cm (½ in.) use hand pruning shears. For branches larger than 4 cm (1½ in.) use a pruning saw. For branches of intermediate size, used lopping shears. If you are pruning a diseased plant, dip the cutting tool in rubbing alcohol after use.

### Shrubs
Shrubs that bloom from buds formed the previous season (azalea, dogwood, lilac, wisteria, climbing roses and rhododendron) should be pruned immediately after flowering. Remove weak and dead branches and lighly prune older ones to make a well-shaped plant.

Remove the flowers of rhododendrons as they pass their prime, just behind the flower head. This will save the plant's energy and ensure new blossoms for the next season.

Shrubs that form their buds from the current season's growth (clematis, cranberry, bush roses, honeysuckle) should be pruned during the dormant season, in winter or early spring.

Neglected shrubs are often full of suckers, riddled with weak growth, or misshapen. They may need to be cut back almost to the ground. This extreme surgery is practised in early spring. Be strong of heart! New tops will sprout from the cut branches during the season and can be thinned to produce a shapely plant.

### Bevel Hedges

Cut hedges so that they are bevelled rather than straight on the sides. The bottom should be 1½ times wider than the top. This will give the lowest branches enough light to keep them healthy. If you let your hedge get too wide at the top it will lose its lower leaves and become "leggy."

### Hedges

Keep hedges trimmed whenever new growth reaches 5-7.5 cm (2-3 in.) throughout the season. Keep shears sharp. Use a string stretched between stakes of equal height as a guide to keep the top of the hedge even and hold the shears flat against the hedge while working.

Cut hedges in a bevel shape rather than trimming them straight up and down. This will permit lower branches to get enough light to keep them thick and healthy. Trim to make the hedge one and half times wider at the bottom than the top.

Trim out dead wood and diseased branches as they appear. Burn the diseased cuttings immediately. Check local ordinances regarding burning and use a barbecue in a pinch.

### Fruit Trees

Young trees can be pruned in midsummer, but more mature trees should be cut back in March or April. During the fruit-bearing years you only need to remove weak or diseased wood, thin the branches and control the height and width of the tree. Do this every year to encourage good-sized, high-colour fruit.

## 2. Fertilizing

All ornamentals like good food, be they flowers, bulbs, shrubs, vines or trees. After planting, use the recommended dose of organic fertilizers, according to your soil test results and the plant's specific requirements. Then mulch with compost around the base for moisture retention and continued feeding. Make sure the mulch does not touch the stems or trunks at the base of your plants, to prevent bacteria and fungus.

**Fruit trees**: fertilize in the early spring or fall after the foliage has dropped, using natural nitrogen sources (fish fertilizer is fantastic). Start with a low dose of 5 m*l* diluted in 23 *l* (1 tsp. in 6 US gal.) of water at planting and increase the concentration by 5 m*l* (1 tsp.) each year, to a maximum of about 1 *l* (1 qt.) for full-size trees and 0.5 *l* (½ qt.) for dwarf varieties. Keep a record of your annual dose. Apply fertilizers well outside the drip line, to ensure nourishment for the roots.

**Evergreen transplant**s enjoy an occasional side-dressing of well-rotted manure or compost in late fall or early winter. Mulch with evergreen boughs, oak leaves and grass cuttings. Check your soil and at the nursery for specific fertilizer needs.

**Lilacs** are heavy feeders and need fertilizing every year. Apply a side dressing of compost under the drip line in spring. Lilacs like acidic soil, so you can apply a mulch of hay, leaves, pine needles or grass clippings, but avoid clippings from pesticide-treated lawns.

NOTE: Make sure to keep a record of the annual dose of fertilizer given to each tree.

### Leaf Them Alone

Fallen leaves are excellent fertilizers. Instead of raking them up and sending them to the dump, leave them on your yard, raking them where you need the most mulch over the winter season.

## 3. Watering

All ornamental plants need water immediately after transplanting. Water the soil, never the foliage.

Good drainage is essential. Make sure you create a slight mound around the trunk of trees when you plant, or leave a slight depression in the soil in a 60-cm (2-ft.) circle to create a well. Mulches can be applied to retain moisture, but should not touch the trunks.

Most tree and shrub species should be watered thoroughly for the first two weeks after transplanting. A soaker hose is perfect for the task. After that, infrequent deep drinks over the season will be sufficient. Plant drought-resistant varieties. As I write, North America is in its fourth to sixth year of drought, depending on the region, and the forecast calls for continuing warm dry weather.

## ROSES

Roses seem to be the most popular plant used in landscaping Canadian and US homes and thus deserve a special section in this book. If your climate is very dry, very damp or severe in winter, choose a native species. You will be planting a species that has evolved over thousands of years to do well in your yard with minimal care, minimal water and minimal pest problems.

**Teas** and **hybrid** tea roses such as the peace and Arlene Francis are favoured for their large single blooms, but they're the the most difficult to keep healthy.

**Floribunda** roses are more disease-resistant and stand up to cold much better. They produce clusters of flowers and bloom throughout the season.

**Grandiflora** varieties like Queen Elizabeth have longer and thicker stems, making them hardier still. Your nursery or catalog will provide you with the choices available in your area. Remember, there are many beautiful native species of rose in North America that have evolved over millennia to be pest-resistant and hardy in their regions.

**Shrub** roses are even hardier and often the most fragrant. They overwinter well in North American climates and may be planted in borders with deciduous shrubbery like Forsythia. They have very attractive but modest-sized blossoms. All the native roses in North America are shrub roses—hint, hint!

When planting roses, dig a trench 60 cm (2 ft.) deep and return the soil, mixed with 125ml (½ cup) of rose food, to the hole. Let the enriched soil rest at least two weeks.

Bring out the rose bush and dig a hole in your prepared trench slightly larger than the diameter of the spread roots and just deep enough to bury the bud graft. Make a cone at the base of the hole with half your soil and gently spread the roots in a skirt over it. Fill in the hole with the rest of the enriched soil. Tamp down, water and let rest.

In climates that have winter temperatures below -12° C (10° F), roses must be protected with 20 cm (8"in.) of soil mounded at the base of the plant well before the first frost.

**Rugosa** roses are a family of vigorous shrubs that produce large fragrant blossoms almost continually through the season. Rugosa roses also attract birds that eat garden bugs. They are resistant to insects and diseases and require no pruning or pampering. They are considered the workhorse of the rose world.

## Planting roses

Roses *are finicky*. They require a lot of attention, even when preparing the planting bed. The first thing to do—after making sure your plant will do well in your soil and climate—is to dig a 60-cm (2-ft.) trench where the rose will go. Save the soil and mix it with 125 m*l* (½ cup) of a special rose food (see below) and return it to the bed, filling the trench to the surface. Allow the prepared soil to settle for two weeks before planting in the spot.

Two weeks later, on an overcast day, or before the sun is hot, examine the roots and cut away any damaged sections. Long and straggly roots should also be cut back and the tips of most others removed.

Dig your hole in the rested trench slightly larger than the diametre of the spread roots and barely deep enough to bury the bud graft. Save all the soil you remove during this digging. Create a cone-shaped mound at the centre of the hole at the desired depth for planting, using roughly half the soil (see illustration on previous page).

Place the rose in the ground, gently spreading the roots in a skirt over the prepared mound. Hold the plant upright, adding some of the remaining soil until the hole is half full. Gently pour in a pail of water. After the water has seeped away, fill the hole with the rest of your soil mix to ground level and tamp down firmly. Water again, gently.

Prune all branches 15-20 cm (6-8 inches) above the soil level. This may seem brutal, but your rose will live a longer, pest-free life as a result.

## Rose maintenance

Most roses—except natives—need lots of water in dry seasons, one of my major objections to their popularity. As our water resources become more scarce and drought conditions more common, we would be well advised to look at a natives-only approach when it comes to roses.

### Rose food: The not-so-secret recipe

This is my own not-so-secret blend for best-blooming healthy roses. In the first edition of this book I decided to share it with the world. Several commercial retailers now distribute it, already prepared; it *is* fabulous:

- 42 percent blood meal
- 36 percent super phosphate or bone meal
- 9.5 percent sulphate of potash
- 7.5 percent kelp meal
- 5 percent sulpomag

When you do water, water the soil, not the foliage. This is especially important with roses as they are susceptible to fungal and bacterial disease if the stems, flowers or leaves are allowed to become moist. Water the soil deeply to the root depth—use a commercially available probe to determine depth of seepage—in the early morning using a drip hose. About an hour should do it.

Organic mulches are great to use in dry, hot areas and landscape fabric is recommended for wetter climates.

Once planted, all roses will love this blend of (5–7–6) rose food made from 42 percent blood meal, 36 percent super phosphate or bone meal, 9.5 percent sulphate of potash, 7.5 percent kelp meal and 5 percent sulpomag. You can make this up yourself or purchase it premixed.

When feeding teas and hybrid teas, gently scrape the soil

at the base of the bush to the drip line with a fork. Sprinkle 125 m*l* (½ cup) of the blend on the area and water gently. Repeat using 190 m*l* (¾ cup) just before or at blooming (late June to early July) and replace mulch if used. Apply 190 m*l* (¾ cup) again in very late fall, after all leaves have dropped and just before you mound your plants for winter protection.

For climbers, bush roses, multifloras and grandifloras, double the above application rates.

Winter protection is essential in most of North America. Where the temperature may fall below -12° C (10° F), mound soil around the plants to a depth of at least 20 cm (8 in.). Draw the canes upright with ties that will not bite into them and trim them all to 75 cm (30 in.). Once the ground is frozen, you may apply mulches of straw, leaves, or garden refuse over the mounded soil. If you live in an area that is likely to experience cold winter winds, a burlap wrap or shield for the canes is advised.

Even in more temperate climates, it is a good idea to mound the bases of your rose plants with leaves or straw as a mulch.

Winter coverings, including mulches, should be removed a couple of weeks after the last frost his passed, before spring growth starts. Let the soil surrounding the plants dry out in the spring sun until summer mulches are needed, to prevent blight.

## Rose diseases

**Black spot**, which looks like its name, is a fungus that attacks the leaves of roses. The spots are actually the spore cells of the disease. All infected leaves should be removed and destroyed immediately, preferably by burning. Fire up the barbecue if necessary.

To prevent black spot, plant roses in full sun and increase air circulation around each bush by pruning. Do not place the plants too close to buildings or each other. Remove organic mulches from the stems and use landscape fabric as a mulch instead. Water the soil, not the leaves, in the early morning and only when necessary.

In fall, rake fallen leaves, grass clippings and other plant debris from around the base of your roses and protect with a mound of soil only. Debris serves as an overwintering home for disease.

If black spot continues to harass your rose, remove it and plant a more appropriate species of ornamental, or a rose that is native to your region.

**Powdery mildew**: Like black spot, this fungus likes overly damp conditions. It is a powdery white growth that covers the tops of leaves as well as young shoots. Infected leaves become twisted and red.

Plant resistant varieties in full sun and observe proper watering practices. Allow your soil to dry almost completely to root level before watering.

Thin out your plants and prune to insure excellent air circulation. Promptly remove and destroy all infected parts. If the fungus persists, plant a native species instead.

For other rose pests, see **Troubleshooting**, below

## ORNAMENTAL PLANT TROUBLESHOOTING
General tips for trees and shrubs

There are many ways to deter pests before they damage your ornamentals. Burlap wrap around the stems of shrubs, vines and trees is a good preventive measure against all crawlers. You can also apply a whitewash made with lime and water or watered-down latex paint to protect tree trunks against sunscald and cold in winter months. Whitewash also repels certain borers and worms.

Prevent worms and caterpillars from crawling to leaves by applying a protective sticky band to the trunks and stems in fall and spring. Use Tree Tanglefoot or another commercially available product made for this purpose. Leave no gaps in the bands for insects to traverse. If you are trapping large numbers of beneficials, rethink your priorities. Remove the tree or shrub and replace it with a native species less prone to pests.

For protection against infestations of aphids, red bug, scale, red spider mites and thrips on most trees and bushes (including roses), spray the entire plant with horticultural oil in early spring before any buds open. The sprays are available at most nursery and gardening supply stores, but some contain highly toxic additives such as sulphur, copper and arsenic. Don't buy them! Spray in early morning to allow proper drying time. Note that oil cannot be used on all tree species; make sure you read the label. Spray again in fall to kill eggs.

Attract pest-eating birds by planting certain flowers (see **Bug-eating birds**, pp. 24-26). Attract beneficial insects such as ladybugs, praying mantis, dragonflies etc. by planting their favourite flowers for food and shelter. They will eat many times their weight in harmful bugs and will stay in your garden as long as there's food for them.

Good housekeeping is essential. Pick up all dropped blossoms and fruit from your flowers, trees and shrubs as they fall. Remove and destroy all diseased growth as soon as it appears, but do not add it to your compost pile.

Monitor your plants weekly for signs of bug infestations, leaf curl, blight and other problems. Commercially available traps for certain pests can be used to capture specimens for identification. Then treat them organically with one of the troubleshooting methods listed below.

**Smothering protection: Horticultural oils**

Dormant or miscible oils can be sprayed on roses, fruit trees and other trees and shrubs to smother overwintering scale, aphids, spider mites and other pests. Some commercially available oils are mixed with sulphur, copper, or arsenic. Read the label and avoid those mixed with these toxic substances.

## Ornamental pests

**Aphids**: Also known as green bugs, these juice-sucking insects love just about any plant and seem to flock to rose bushes. High nitrogen levels in soil and plant tissue attract several aphid species. Put away the highly nitrogenized chemical fertilizers. Check your soil and amend accordingly with slow-releasing organic fertilizers.

Gently rub infested leaves between your thumb and fingers to squish the aphids. Aphids shy away from plants mulched with a layer of heavy aluminum foil. Place a large circular disk of foil flat on the ground around the trunk or stem.

Plant "trap crops," flowers that aphids love even more than roses. Nasturtiums seem to be aphids' favourite food, so plant some a few feet away from your infested flowers and the aphids will concentrate on this treat.

You could buy beneficial nematodes, but these need lots of water to remain active, so I don't recommend this practice. Natural predators include ladybugs, praying mantis, parasitic wasps, house finches, warblers and bushtits. Don't buy beneficials—attract them to your yard by providing the plants they like for food and shelter.

**Wound Woes**
When mowing, edging, or pruning around ornamentals, be careful not to wound your plants. Bugs will use any cuts in the bark as points of entry.

**Borers**: Borer larvae tunnel into stems and trunks, weakening and eventually killing plants. Borers are indiscriminate: they like apple, ash, azalea, dogwood, flowering cherry, laurel, lilac, maple, oak, peach, plum, poplar, iris, dahlia, roses and willow trees.

Make sure that the plant you purchase is uninfected, then take preventive measures. Wrap young trees with burlap and waxed freezer paper and renew their wrap as necessary for at least two years after transplanting. Place an unbroken band of a sticky substance such as Tree Tanglefoot around the base of trees to prevent the borers from crawling up the trunk.

Keep your garden clean. Borers overwinter in plant debris and weeds.

Borers gain entry through wounds, so be careful with your tools and lawn mowers. If you cause a wound, scrape it clean and treat with a tree dressing or pruning paint, available at your gardening centre.

Encourage the presence of woodpeckers, crows, vireos and wasps, all of which destroy their share of borers.

**Canker worms and loopers**: These crawlers are recognizable by their characteristic form of locomotion. They extend forward then pull their hind body up in a loop.

Canker worms and loopers attack fruit and shade trees in spring and fall. Apply a sticky band such as Tree Tanglefoot, Tack-Trap, or Stick'em around the trunk to keep the females from climbing up to lay their eggs in February and October. Make sure there are no gaps in the circle.

**Tent caterpillars**: The tent caterpillar spins a familiar tentlike nest in the branches of apple, flowering cherry and other deciduous trees. Your best defence is to remove the tents with a pole and burn them as soon as they appear. Once the caterpillars reach a length of 2.5 cm (1 in.) they stay out to play at night, making them hard to control.

Remove the tents at night, when most caterpillars are inside seeking shelter. The exposed caterpillars will fall prey to local predators

Prune twigs bearing brown, hard, foamy egg collars in winter or very early spring.

**Gypsy moths**: The larvae of this moth are responsible for damage to fruit, ornamental and shade trees. The brown, hairy caterpillar grows to 5 cm (2 in.) and feeds nocturnally through June and July.

To control, wrap burlap around the trunk of your tree in several lengths and fold over the top to form a shelter. Caterpillars will be attracted to the sheltered area when it is time to pupate. Crush the caterpillars inside the band, or remove the burlap and shake pests into bucket of water topped with soap.

Scrape off the tan egg clusters, which are laid in 2.5-cm (1-in.) ovals on branches

## Leafhoppers

These are small, wedge-shaped, winged insects that pierce plant tissue and suck sap, causing weakness and pale colour. A few of the more common to attack ornamentals are:

**Aster leafhopper**, also named **six-spotted leafhopper**, is greenish-yellow with six dark spots and grows to 3 mm (⅛ in.). Asters under attack from these insects will turn brown and die. Aster leafhoppers prefer weedy, open areas and live in surrounding weeds over the winter. In very early spring, remove or burn off weeds, or grow your asters under landscape netting.

**Beet leafhopper,** also known as **whitefly**, is pale yellowish-green and also reaches 3 mm (⅛ in.). It like beets and other vegetable greens, but also loves many flowers, producing a condition known as "curly top": pronounced veins, curled brittle leaves and stunted growth. Your best defence is to plant resistant varieties and remove affected plants as soon as the condition appears.

**Potato leafhopper**, a wedge-shaped green insect with white spots on the head and throat, also loves dahlias. The condition it causes is known as "hopper burn." The leaves of the infected plant curl up, turn yellow and become brittle. The best defence is resistant varieties.

## Leaf Rollers

These caterpillars attack fruit trees and roses, causing the leaves to roll up as they feed. Spray the plant with horticultural oil before the buds open, as outlined in the prevention section. Remove affected branches if the damage is not too widespread and destroy them.

**Fruit tree leaf rollers:** Green caterpillars 1.9 cm (¾ in.) long with black heads. The adult moths are brown and gold. They like apple, apricot, blackberry, cherry, gooseberry, pear, plum, raspberry and shade trees. Spray trees with dormant oil just before the buds break.

**Oblique-banded leaf rollers**: Green caterpillars with black heads that lay eggs on branches of roses, asters, geraniums and carnations. Remove and destroy affected plants and replace with other plant species.

## Leaf Miners

These are insect larvae that tunnel between top and bottom leaf surfaces on apple, birch, blackberry, boxwood, elm, holly, chrysanthemum, columbine, larkspur and roses. As they tunnel, tissue damage causes the leaves to become yellow and blotched.

All infested foliage must be removed and destroyed, the area kept weed-free and well cultivated. Choose resistant varieties.

**Cedar leaf miners**: Not a "true" miner, the larvae of this insect feed on foliage tips of white cedars, causing them to turn brown. Adults are tiny grey moths which take flight when foliage is disturbed in June and July. Clip infested hedges and small bushes before June. Destroy the clippings, burning them where municipal ordinances permit. (The barbecue may come in handy for this task.) This reduces the population before the adults emerge. Leaf miners seldom cause significant damage. Clipping is usually sufficient control.

## Mites

Tiny relatives of the spider family, these insects have two segments in their bodies and no antennae.

**Cyclamen mites**: These are microscopic and like new leaves and blossoms. A sign of their presence is distorted or swollen tissue at infestation sites. The best prevention is good housekeeping, lots of room between each plant for good air circulation and crop rotation.

**European red mites**: These are visible only with the help of a magnifying glass. Then you'll see a dark red insect with white spots. It loves apple, pear and plum trees, feeding on the leaves and changing their colour to bronze. Use dormant oil in the early spring to kill overwintering eggs. Plant resistant varieties.

**Spider mites**: These appear as tiny red dots on the undersides of leaves, discolouring and eventually killing them. They like evergreens, shrubs, ivy and roses. Hose off your plants (except roses) to wash them away and destroy their webs.

## Scale Insects

Many different species of these minute insects attack stems, branches and trunks of ornamental plants in Canada and the United States. Spray dormant oil in late April. Like aphids, they secrete sugars from their host plant, attracting ants and mould.

**Black scale**: Looks like its name. It likes fruit trees, flowers, ornamental trees and shrubs. The resulting mould on infected plants actually blocks the sun from plant tissue, stunting growth.

**Oystershell scale**: This grayish-brown insect prefers deciduous trees and shrubs. Your best defence is to scrape the bark to remove the scale and spray dormant oil in the spring.

## Diseases

Most bacterial, viral and fungal diseases can be kept in check by planting flowers, shrubs and trees in their preferred soil and climate conditions. Overly damp beds with poor drainage and air circulation invite diseases and should be avoided unless you are planting specimens that love all that extra moisture. Plant with adequate airflow in mind and not too close to buildings or fences. Do not use chemical fertilizers or pesticides—they can destroy the microscopic "police" organisms that naturally control bacteria and fungi. Rotate your crops and plant resistant varieties.

If signs of disease appear, immediately remove and destroy all affected growth. Remove organic mulches from around the base of the plant to allow air to get at the roots. If disease persists, call it a day, remove those plant varieties and plant resistant varieties, or better yet, go native.

## THE FINAL WORD

Beautiful landscaping helps to make a house your home. If you grow organically, you won't have to worry about keeping pets or family members off your grounds for fear of pesticide contact.

If you have hired a lawn care service to take care of your lawn, flowers, trees and shrubs, talk to your contractor about the methods outlined in this book and insist that your grounds be maintained without pesticides. Many companies are starting to offer organic service, so shop around if your current contractor seems less than enthusiastic.

Make sure to examine the fine print for the "organic" program being offered, to determine just what the contractor means when using the word. There is no legal definition when it comes to landscaping services, so it really is buyer beware. Give a copy of this book to your landscape contractor, discuss the ideas in it, write a contract based on pesticide-free gardening, then go to it.

You can ask your provincial or state Landscape Association which of their members provide pesticide-free services (the more you contact a Landscaping Association, the more the pesticide-using services will realize there's a new market out there) or check with the local environmental group working on this issue. I have listed several public and private environmental, municipal, provincial and state information contacts in the **Resources** section.

If finding a contractor who will use pesticide-free good horticultural practices to take care of your yard seems daunting, don't give up. Remember, money talks! That is what has changed the product line in millions of nurseries throughout Canada and the United States since 1990—people like you who have decided to make a change in how you live your lives and spend your dollars and who are willing to demand the necessary products and services until the change is possible. Organic fertilizers are now available at department stores across the continent, where only a decade ago customers were laughed at if they requested such items.

You did that. You can do it with organic lawn-care service providers and high-end grass cultivars, too.

All that is needed for beautiful pesticide-free lawns and gardens is a selection of healthy, hardy plants that are appropriate to your yard, and then excellent maintenance. It's simple!

# RESOURCES

Since this book first came out in 1990 the availability of organic lawn-care products has skyrocketed. Most products used in organic gardening and lawn care can now be found at large department, hardware and grocery stores—not to mention your local nursery.

This is a great thing: Money and demand has talked!

If your local outlet is behind in its efforts, some gentle persuasion will most likely get things going.

The following list of contacts, groups and service providers is for your information only. This is not an endorsement of any of the following, but simply a service so that you can pick up the telephone or go on-line when you've finished reading this book and, hopefully, find the information and services you want.

Be sure to get a clear and complete description—in writing- of any lawn/garden service before you hire: the word "organic" means vastly different things to different folks.

## Soil-testing labs, Canada

**Note**: the Woods End lab in Maine is a leader in organic research and provides only organic soil test results. Even better, they now take soil from anywhere in North America. So I am listing them first under both Canada and the US, just to show my support and to encourage you to go directly to the horse's mouth when it comes to testing your soil for organic care.

Some of the other labs listed will provide organic results (i.e. interpreted in a way that will tell you how much of each organic fertilizer source you will need) on request. So, request! If the lab you call won't do the work for you, look elsewhere (and please tell them, respectfully, why you are doing so, to help them get with the program.)

All labs will give you detailed instructions on how to collect soil samples and send them in. Be sure to check on fees before you go ahead.

Woods End Research Laboratory
P.O. Box 297
Mount Vernon ME 04352
207-293-2457
*info@woodsend.org*
*www.woodsend.org*

### British Columbia

Norwest Labs
#104, 19575–55A Ave.
Surrey BC V3S 8P8
800-899-1433
604-514-3322
*www.norwestlabs.com*

Griffin Labs Corp.
#2–2550 Acland Rd.
Kelowna BC V1X 7L4
800-661-2339
*brogers@grifflabs.com*
*www.grifflabs.com*

### Alberta

Norwest Labs
Edmonton Environmental Lab
9938–67 Ave.
Edmonton. AB T6E 0P5
800-661-7645
780-438-5522
*info@norwestlabs.com*
*www.norwestlabs.com*

### Saskatchewan

Enviro Test Lab Ag Services
124 Veterinary Rd.
Saskatoon SK S7N 5E3
800-667-7645

Saskatchewan Soil Testing
Department of Soil Science

General Purpose Building
U of Saskatchewan
Saskatoon SK S7N 0W0
306-966-6890
(will give organic results)

## Manitoba
Norwest Labs
Ag. Services Complex 203
545 University Cres.
Winnipeg MB R3T 5S6
204-982-8630
*www.norwestlabs.com*

Manitoba Provincial Soil
Testing Lab
Department of Soil Sciences
U of Manitoba
Winnipeg MB R3T 2N2
204-474-8153
*soilscience@umanitoba.ca*

## Ontario
Nutrite
Box 160
Elmira ON N3B 2Z6
519-669-5401
800-265-8865
(will give organic results)

OMAFRA
Box 8000
Vineland Stn. ON L0R 2E0
905-562-4147
(will provide a list of
Ontario labs)

## Quebec
Soil Test Lab
Rm. MS2–099,
Macdonald-Steward Bldg.
Macdonald Campus of McGill U
21–111 Lakeshore Rd.
Ste-Anne-de-Bellevue QC
H9X 3V9
514-398-7890

Agriculture and AgriFood Canada
Sainte-Foy Research Station
2560 Hochelaga Blvd.
Sainte-Foy, QC G1V 2J3
418-657-7980
(not a government soil-testing
agency—Quebec has none—but
an information resource)

## Nova Scotia
Laboratory Services
Quality Evaluation Division
Nova Scotia Department of
Agriculture & Fisheries
P.O. Box 550
Truro NS B2N 5E3
902-893-7444
(will give organic results)
*Larusima@gov.ns.ca*
*www.gov.ns.ca/nsaf*

## Prince Edward Island
PEI Soil & Feed Testing Lab
PO Box 1600
Research Station
Charlottetown PEI C1A 7N3
866-734-3276
902-368-5628
(will give organic results)

## Newfoundland & Labrador
Soil Plant and Feed Laboratory
Dept. of Forest Resources and
Agrifoods
Provincial Agriculture Building
PO Box 8700
Brookfield Road St. John's NL
A1B 4J6
709-729-6738

# Soil-Testing Labs, US

The following is a list of soil testing labs put together from every source I could find. Contact the lab to find out how what they charge, whether they will give results for organic gardening (i.e., organic-sourced fertilizers) and how they want you to collect and send in specimens.

Again, I have listed Woods End lab first, because of their great, organic reputation. After that, listings are by state, alphabetically. Some offer organic services, some don't. If the one you contact doesn't, shop elsewhere and tell them why.

Woods End Research Laboratory
P.O. Box 297
Mount Vernon ME 04352
207-293-2457
*www.woodsend.org*
*info@woodsend.org*

## Alabama
Soil-testing Lab
118 Funchess hall
Auburn University, AL
36849–5411
334-844-3958

## Alaska
U of Alaska, Fairbanks
Agriculture & Forestry
Experiment Station Lab
Palmer Research Center
533 E. Fireweed Ave.
Palmer, AK 99645
907-746-9482

## Arizona
No government or university testing service. For a list of
commercial testing labs, check
*http://ag.arizona.edu/pubs/*
*garden/az1111.pdf*

## Arkansas
Soil Testing and Research Lab
U of Arkansas
PO Drawer 767
Marianna, AR 72360
870-295-2851

## California
No government or university
testing service. For info contact:
U of California
California Master Gardeners
Network
21150 Box Springs Rd.
Moreno Valley CA 92557
909-683-6491

## Colorado
Soil Water & Plant Testing Lab
Natural & Environmental sciences
Bldg, Rm. A319
Colorado State University
Fort Collins, CO 80523–1120
970-491-5061

## Connecticut
Soil Testing Lab
U of C
2019 Hillside Rd.
Storrs CT 06269–1102
860-486-2928

## Delaware
Soil Testing Program
Dept. of Plant & Soil Sciences
U of Delaware
Newark, DE 19717–1303
302-831-1392

## Florida
Soil Testing Lab IFAS
631 Wallace Bldg.,
U of Florida
Gainesville, FL 32611–0740
325-392-1950
*soilslab@mail.ifas.ufl.edu*

## Georgia
Soil, Plant & Water Analysis Lab
U of Georgia
2400 College Station Rd.
Athens GA 30602–4356
706-542-5350

## Hawaii
Agricultural Diagnostic Center
College of Tropical Agriculture
and Human Resources
U of Hawaii at Manoa
1910 East-West Rd.  Rm. 134
Honolulu HI 96822
808-956-6706

## Idaho
Analytical Science Lab
Holm Research Center
U of Idaho
Moscow, ID 83844–2203
208-885-7081
*www.its.uidaho.edu/asl*

## Illinois
Universal Analytical Lab Inc.
15006 State Rte 127 North
Carlyle IL 62231
618-594-2627
*www.ualab.com*
*ualab@ualab.com*

and follow links)

## Indiana
A&L Great Lakes Labs Inc.
3505 Conestoga Dr.
Fort Wayne IN 46808–4413
260-483-4759
*www.algreatlakes.com*

## Iowa
Iowa State University
Soil Testing Lab
G501 Agronomy Hall
Ames IA 50011
515-294-3076

## Kansas
Soil Testing Labs
Throckmorton Hall Rm. 2308
Kansas State U
Manhattan KS 66506–5504
785-532-7897

## Kentucky
U of Kentucky Soil Testing Labs
103 Regulatory Service Bldg.
U of Kentucky
Lexington, KY 40546–0275
phone 859-257-2785
*fsikora@uky.edu*

## Louisiana
Soil Testing Lab
126 Madison B. Sturgis Hall
Louisiana State U
Baton Rouge LA 70803
225-578-1261
*www.lsuagcenter.com*
*/stpalstpal@agcenter.lsu.edu*

## Maine
Maine Soil Testing Service
5722 Deering Hall, U of Maine
Orono ME 04469–5722
207-581-3591
*http://anlab.umesci.maine.edu*

## Maryland
Soil Testing Lab
0225 H.J. Patterson Hall
U of Maryland
College Park, MD 20742
301-405-1349
*www.nrsl.umd.edu*
(click on "Extension & Outreach"

## Massachusetts
Soil Testing Lab
West Experiment Station
U of Massachusetts
Amherst MA 01003–8020
413-545-2311
*www.umass.edu/plsoils/soiltest/*
*soiltesting@hotmail.com*

## Michigan
Soil & Plant Nutrient Lab
Plant & Soil Sciences Building,
Rm. A81
Michigan State U
East Lansing MI 48824–1325
517-355-0218
*dahl@msu.edu*

## Minnesota
Soil Testing Lab
U of Minnesota
Rm. 135 Crops Research Bldg.
1902 Dudley Ave
St. Paul MN 55108–6089
612-625-3101
*soiltest@soils.umn.edu*
*http://soiltest.coafes.umn.edu*

## Mississippi
Soil Testing Lab
Box 9610
Mississippi State U, MS 39762
662-325-3313

## Missouri
Soil Testing Lab
23 Mumford Hall
U of Missouri
Columbia MO 65211
573-882-0623
*SoilTestingServices@missouri.edu*
*www.soiltest.psu.missouri.edu*

## Montana
No government or university test-
ing service. For information
contact:
Land Resources & Environmental
Sciences
Montana State University

Bozeman, MT 59717
406-994-3515
(MSU does not provide soil testing to the home gardener, but can provide a list of private soil testing labs.)

### Nebraska
Soil & Plant Lab
U of Nebraska
139 Keim Hall
Lincoln NE 68583–1571
402-472-1571

### Nevada
No public or private soil-testing agency, apart from landscape companies that use pesticides and chemical fertilizers, could be confirmed as this book went to press.

### New Hampshire
Soil Testing Lab
U of New Hampshire
Spaulding Life Science Center
Rooms G-54 and 55
38 College Rd.
Durham NH 03824
603-862-3210 or 3212
*soiltesting@unh.edu*

### New Jersey
Rutgers Soil Testing Lab
P.O. Box 902
Milltown NJ 08850
732-932-9295

### New Mexico
New Mexico State University
Soil Water & Air Testing Lab
Box 30003, Dept. 3Q
Las Cruces, NM 88003
505-646-4422

### New York
Cornell Nutrient Analysis Lab
804 Bradfield Hall
Cornell U
Ithaca NY 14853
607-255-4540
*soiltest@cornell.edu*

### North Carolina
NC Dept of Agriculture
Soil Testing Section
4300 Reedy Creek Rd.
Raleigh NC 27607
919-733-2655

### North Dakota
Soil Testing Lab
103 Waldron Hall
North Dakota State U
P.O. Box 5575
Fargo ND 58105
701-231-9589

### Ohio
No government or university testing service found. Ohio State University has advice on selecting a lab on its website at *http://ohioline.osu.edu/hyg-fact/1000/1133.html.*

Brookside Labs
308 S. Main St.
New Knoxville OH 45871
419-753-2448
(also accredited in Ontario)

### Oklahoma
Oklahoma State U
Soil, Water & Forage Lab
048 Agriculture Hall
Stillwater OK 74078
405-744-6630
*soils_lab@mail.pss.okstate.edu*

### Oregon
No government or university testing service found. A list of private soil analysts may be found at *http://eesc.orst.edu/agcomwebfile/EdMat/html/em/em8677/em8677.html*

Soil Foodweb Inc.
1128 NE 2nd St. Suite 120
Corvallis, OR 97330
541-752-5006
*info@soilfoodweb.com*

**Pennsylvania**
Agricultural Analytical
Services Lab
Penn State U
University Park, PA 16802
814-863-0841
*aaslab@psu.edu*
*www.aasl.psu.edu*

**Rhode Island**
See Massachusetts. Soil testing is
no longer performed at URI.

**South Carolina**
Agriculture Service Lab
Clemson U
171 Old Cherry Rd.
Clemson, SC 29634–0313
864-656-2068
*kmr@clemson.edu*
*http://virtual.clemson.edu*
*/groups/agsrvlb/*

**South Dakota**
Soil Testing Lab
Box 2207 A
South Dakota State U
Brookings SD 57007–1096
605-688-4766
*Ronald_Gelderman@sdstate.edu*
*http://plantsci.sdstate.edu*
*/woodardh/soiltest*

**Tennessee**
U of Tennessee Soil testing lab
5201 Marchant Drive
Nashville TN 37211–5112
615-832-5850
*djoines2@utk.edu*
*http://bioengr.ag.utk.edu*
*/SoilTestLab*

**Texas**
Texas A&M University
Soil, Water & Forage
Testing Lab
Rm. 345, Heep Center
College Station TX 77843–2474
409-845-4816
*http://soiltesting.tamu.edu*

**Utah**
Soil Testing Lab
Utah State U
Logan, UT 84322–4830
435-797-2217
*http://extension.usu.edu/*
*publica/gardpubs/hfs05.pdf*

**Vermont**
UVM Ag & Environmental
Testing Lab
219 Hills Bldg
U of Vermont
Burlington VT 05405
802-656-3030
800-244-6402
*ecarr@zoo.uvm.edu*
*http://pss.uvm.edu/ag_testing/*
*soil.html*

**Virginia**
Virginia Tech Soil Testing Lab
145 Smyth Hall 0465
Blacksburg VA 24161
540-231-6893

**West Virginia**
Soil Testing Lab
1090 Agricultural Sciences Bldg
West Virginia U
Morgantown, WV 26506–6108
304-293-6023

**Wisconsin**
Soil & Plant Analysis Lab
U of Wisconsin–Madison
5711 Mineral Point Rd.
Madison WI 53705
608-262-4364
*http://uwlab.soils.wisc.edu/*

**Wyoming**
Soil Testing Lab
Renewable Resources
U of Wyoming
P.O. Box 3354
Laramie WY 82071
307-766-2135
*soiltest@uwyo.edu*

# Organic landscaping services

Because a directory of pesticide-free yard care providers proved unwieldy, I invite you to contact local environmental groups to ask for references to pesticide-free contractors. You can also contact your state, provincial and regional landscape associations and municipal parks and recreation departments for referrals. This will help to carry the message to business and government that these services are needed.

# Information sources/contacts

## Canada
### Nationwide
Sierra Club of Canada
*www.sierraclub.ca* (home page, links to provincial chapters)
*www.sierraclub.ca/national/pest/index.html* (information on pesticides)

Green Communities Association, Canadian
headquarters:
Box 928 Peterborough ON
K9J 7A5
705-745-7479
*cmaynes@gca.ca*
*www.gca.ca* (Links to local environmental and ecological groups across Canada.)

### Western and Northern Canada
IPM Handbook
(excellent, free download)
By Dr. Linda Gilkeson

B.C. Government, Water, Land & Air Protection
*www.gov.bc.ca*
Click: Ministries and Organizations
click: Water land & air protection

click: Integrated Pest Management
click: Publications & resources
click:IPM Manuals

Manitoba Eco-Network
2–70 Albert Street, Winnipeg MB R3B 1E7
204-947-6511
*mbeconet@mts.net*
*www.web.ca/men*

Saskatchewan Environmental Society
203–115 2nd Ave. N. Saskatoon, SK S7K 2B1
306-665-1915
*saskenv@link.ca*
*www.lights.com/ses*

Arctic Energy Alliance
101–5102 51st St., Yellowknife, NT, X1A 3S8
867-920-3333
*info@aea.nt.ca*
*www.aea.nt.ca*

### Central Canada
City of Toronto Parks & Recreation Healthy Lawns Program
*www.city.toronto.on.ca/parks/healthylawn*

Toronto Environmental Alliance
201-30 Duncan St.
Toronto, ON
MV5 2C3
416-596-0660
*tea@torontoenvironment.org*
*www.torontoenvironment.org*

Organic Landscape Alliance
30 Duncan St.
416-496-7989
*info@organiclandscape.org*
*www.organiclandscape.org*

Nature-Action Québec
CP 434, St. Bruno QC J3V 5G8
450-441-3899
*info@nature-action.qc.ca*
*www.nature-action.qc.ca*

## Atlantic Canada
Conservation Corps of
Newfoundland and Labrador
Box 37012, St. John's NL
A1E 1B5
709-758-7330
*speckford@conservationcorps.
nf.ca*
*www.conservationcorps.nf.ca*

Clean Nova Scotia Home
Tune-Up
126 Portland St., Dartmouth NS
B2Y 1H8
902-420-3474
*cns@clean.ns.ca*
*www.clean.ns.ca*

Halifax Regional Municipality
*www.region.halifax.ns.ca/
pesticides*

## United States
## Nationwide
Beyond Pesticides
(formerly National Coalition
Against the Misuse of Pesticides,
NCAMP)
701 E Street S.E. #200
Washington, D.C. 20003
202-543-5450
*info@beyondpesticides.org*
*www.beyondpesticides.org*

Pesticide Action Network
North America
49 Powell St., Suite 500,
San Francisco CA 94102
415-981-1771
*panna@panna.org*
*www.panna.org*

The above both have links to local
groups in most states.

National Turfgrass
Evaluation Program
10300 Baltimore Ave.
Bldg. 003, Rm. 218
Beltsville Agricultural Research
Centre-West
Beltsville, Maryland 20705
301-504-5125
*kmorris@ntep.org*
*www.ntep.org*

Sierra Club
*www.sierraclub.com*

## Western US
Californians for Alternatives
to Toxics
315 P St., Eureka CA 95501
707-445-5100
*cats@alternatives2toxics.org*
*www.alternatives2toxics.org*

Arizona Toxics
P.O. Box 1896, Bisbee AZ 86603
602-432-7340

Northwest Coalition for
Alternatives to Pesticides (NCAP)
PO Box 1393 Eugene, OR
97440–1393
541-344-5044
*info@pesticide.org*
*www.pesticide.org*

## Central US
Safer Pest Control Project (SPCP)
25 E. Washington St, Suite 1515,
Chicago, IL 60602
312-641-5575
*spcp@iname.com*
*www.spcpweb.org*

Kids for Saving the Earth
PO Box 421118
Minneapolis, MN 55442
Phone:763-559-1234
*kseww@aol.com*
*www.kidsforsavingearth.org*

## Eastern US
Maryland Pesticide Network
533 Epping Forest Rd.
Annapolis MD 21401
410-849-3909
*info@dmpestnet.org*
*www.mdpestnet.org*

New York Coalition for
Alternatives to Pesticides
353 Hamilton St., Albany NY
12210–1709
518-426-8246
*nycap@crisny.org*
*www.crisny.org/
not-for-profit/nycap*

# FURTHER READING:

Bull, John and Farrand, John Jr. *The Audubon Society Field Guide to North American Birds, Eastern Region*. New York: Alfred A. Knopf, 1994

Bradley, F. M. and Ellis, Barbara, editors. *Rodale's All New Encyclopedia of Organic Gardening*, Revised Edition. Emmaus, PA: Rodale Press, 1993.

Ellis, Barbara and Tenenbaum, Francis, editors. *Safe and Easy Lawn Care: The Complete Guide to Organic, Low Maintenance Lawns*. Boston: Houghton Mifflin, 1997

Harris, Marjorie. *Ecological Gardening: Your Path to a Healthy Garden*. New York: Random House, 1991.

Milne, Lorus and Milne, Lorus J. *The Audubon Society Field Guide to North American Insects and Spiders*. New York: Alfred A. Knopf, 1980

Nancarrow, Loren and Taylor, Janet Hogan. *Dead Daisies Make Me Crazy: Garden Solutions Without Chemical Pollution*. Berkeley, CA: Ten Speed Press, 2000.

Olkowski, William, Daar, Sheila and Olkowski, Helga. *Common Sense Pest Control*. Newtown, CT: Taunton Press, 1991.

Raymond, Dick. *Down to Earth Natural Lawn Care*. North Adams, MA: Storey Books, 1993

Riotte, Louise. *Carrots Love Tomatoes*. North Adams, MA: Storey Books, 1998.

Rubin, Carole. *How To Get Your Lawn Off Grass, A North American Guide To Turning Off The Water Tap And Going Native*. Madeira Park, BC: Harbour Publishing, 2002

Udvardy, Miklos D.F. *The Audubon Society Field Guide to North American Birds, Western Region*. Revised by John Farr

# Index